Natal
PROVINCE OF CONTRASTS

Natal PROVINCE OF CONTRASTS

Gerald Cubitt & David Steele
Text: David Barritt

Published by Don Nelson
Cape Town 1981

First edition 1981
Copyright photography Gerald Cubitt & David Steele
ISBN 0 909238 68 5
Designed by Peter Ibbotson
Photoset by Unifoto (Pty) Ltd., Cape Town
Lithographic reproduction by McManus Bros. (Pty) Ltd., Cape Town
Printed by Printpak (Cape) Ltd., Cape Town

Introduction

Natal is a land blessed with great beauty, fertile soil, a magnificent coastline and a rich diversity of people. The smallest of South Africa's four provinces, it is nevertheless home to 20% of all South Africans.

Sandwiched between Mozambique to the north and Transkei to the south, Natal is famed for its unspoilt wilderness areas and reserves rich in wildlife, and also for some of the most spectacular mountains in the world: the formidable Drakensberg.

The history of Natal is also rather wild and thorny, from the early clashes between Bushman and Nguni, to a destructive struggle for possession between Zulu, Boer and Briton which led to several wars and many historic confrontations. These are commemorated – not so much for monuments to victory, as reminders of the bloody consequences of man's inability to live with man.

After tracing its history and discussing every aspect of this land of contrasts, this book attempts for the first time to take the reader on a comprehensive visual tour of South Africa's unique multi-faceted province of Natal.

Talented photographers Gerald Cubitt and David Steele begin their journey in the majestic Drakensberg which many regard as one of the wonders of South Africa. From the Drakensberg we travel inland to Pietermaritzburg, the central city of the Midlands, rich in history and tradition.

We visit the congenial holiday havens of the South Coast and then move on to Durban itself which is a hub of industry – the busiest seaport in Southern Africa – and of lively holiday pleasure. The hotels, amusement parks, discos, cinemas, restaurants and shops keep up a pace that outstrips the more staid and sober remainder of the country.

Before entering the Natal Game Parks, we meet the proud Zulu people who once controlled one of the mightiest empires in Africa and dominated the continent south of the Sahara with their formidable military machine.

The entire area of Natal was once a giant natural game reserve but the advent of White settlers took a heavy toll on the wildlife, and today to see wild animals requires a journey to a game reserve. Fortunately Natal has superb reserves and Cubitt and Steele linger extensively in Ndumu, Mkuzi, St Lucia, Hluhluwe and Umfolozi.

The true magnificence of Natal is vividly portrayed in this rich portfolio by two master photographers.

Vasco da Gama, the Portuguese navigator-explorer who named Natal on Christmas Day, 1497, on his way to India. (Cape Archives)

Historical Sketch

Natal owes its name to the determination of a fifteenth century European king to find a sea route to India. King John II of Portugal ordered the construction of a fleet of ships which were to travel round Africa to discover if there was a way to reach the land of precious spices by sea and thus render Portugal free of the expensive and troublesome middle-men who dominated the overland route.

John died before the ships were completed but his successor, King Manuel I, continued with the project and in 1495 despatched Vasco da Gama in command of three wooden ships on what was to become an extremely famous voyage. Da Gama sailed south from Lisbon along the west coast of Africa until he reached the Cape Verde Islands; then he headed west, sailing far out into the Atlantic Ocean before swinging back in a great arc to arrive at the African coast near the Cape of Good Hope.

Even today the treacherous waters off the Cape are feared by sailors but da Gama managed to steer his little fleet through the heavy seas, rounded the Cape and continued his voyage northwards in the warm Indian Ocean, along the east coast of Africa.

On Christmas Day 1497, on board the *San Rafael*, he was sailing past a harbourless coast along which sand and rock beaches alternated and beyond which he could see rolling wooded hills. Da Gama named the land Natal to honour the birth of Christ. There is no evidence that da Gama actually set foot in Natal but he did reach India and returned a hero to Portugal in ships loaded with spice.

Once da Gama had proved that the sea route was practicable other Portuguese navigators made use of it and in the years that followed a number of ships nosed their way up and down the Natal coast. Inevitably there were wrecks. On 24th June, 1552 the *St John*, a great Portuguese galleon loaded with treasure, was wrecked off the mouth of the Umzimvubu River, in a place called today Port St Johns in remembrance of the disaster.

500 people survived the wreck and, led by the ship's captain, Dom Manuel de Souza, set out to walk along the coast to the nearest Portuguese settlement at Sofala, several hundred kilometres north. De Souza's wife, Donna Leonora de Souza, and her two small sons were the first White woman and children to set foot in Natal. Sadly, only a handful of survivors ever reached Sofala and the De Souzas were not among them. Donna Leonora and the children died on the arduous journey and Dom Manuel was so overcome with grief that he rushed off into the bush and was never seen again.

In the years that followed the wreck of the *St John*, shipwrecks landed around 3000 people on the Natal coast. Barely 500 were ever rescued. Most died of hunger or from encounters with the wild animals which roamed throughout the territory, or at the hands of hostile tribes. A lucky few met friendly local tribes and were incorporated into tribal life; when they were encountered in later years by other shipwreck-survivors some of these men had forgotten their original language.

Although credit for discovering Natal from the sea goes to da Gama it is likely that credit truly belongs to the Phoenicians who may have made a similar voyage some 2000 years earlier. In 610 BC the Phoenician Pharo Necho sent out an expedition to circumnavigate Africa from east to west. The Greek historian Herodotus records that the expedition completed its task by travelling down the east coast and returning to the northern hemisphere along the west African coast, re-entering the Mediterranean sea via 'The Pillars of Hercules', Ceuta and Gibraltar.

Certainly Natal was inhabited thousands of years before da Gama arrived. Pre-humans lived there in the distant past and when they died out their place was taken by Stone Age hunter-gatherer people called Bushmen who left evidence of their period of tenure in a wealth of rock paintings in the Drakensberg mountains. Natal at the time of the Bushmen was teeming with wild life. All sorts of animals from lumbering elephants to darting monkeys filled the territory from the sea to the mountains.

When da Gama passed Natal it was a giant natural game reserve. But new human owners were already on their way to take possession: the Bantu people. The origin of these dark-skinned people is unknown but they had begun migrating southwards from North Africa thousands of years previously.

Bantu culture was centred around cattle and their migrations followed the paths of the slow-moving beasts. The Bantu eddied around Africa, moving this way and that, but always their impetus carried them south. By the 14th century they were south of the Zambesi, and by the 16th century they were living in what is today the Transvaal. An off-shoot of these people filtered down through the high Drakensberg mountains into the coastal strip beyond, part of present day Natal. The lure of uncrowded, well-watered grazing for the all-important cattle ensured that the migration to Natal was speedy and the migrants numerous.

The Bantu people who settled in Natal are generally described as Nguni, a classification derived from the languages they speak. The Nguni people had already settled in parts of Natal when the Hollander, Jan van Riebeeck, was founding South Africa's first White settlement in the Cape in 1652. The larger Bantu group to which the Nguni belong continued their relentless movement south, and in the latter part of the century they collided with the thrust of the White settlers moving northwards. Almost from the first meeting the two groups, to their mutual surprise, discovered that their destiny was inextricably interwoven. It was a shotgun wedding if you like, but as there was no more land for either group to move on to, it was a wedding without the possibility of divorce, and yet the two groups had compatibility problems from the start.

The Whites, accustomed to the less well-organised Bushmen and Hottentots of the Cape, thought themselves superior to all Black people and they did not understand or appreciate the semi-nomadic, rootless life-style of the Blacks. The Bantu for their part had no understanding at all of White society or of White concepts of land ownership. The problems caused by this clash of cultures were not felt severely in Natal in the very early days of the territory because the few White people living there were concentrated around the site of the modern city of Durban. The reason for this is that behind a promontory of land which projects out into the sea at this point lies a secure place for ships to shelter, a rarity on South Africa's East coast. The Portuguese knew of the harbour and all subsequent mariners made it an important stopping place for shelter and water.

On 9th May, 1685 a British ship called the *Good Hope* was wrecked when trying to cross the sand bar barring the harbour's entrance. 18 people survived and they became the first Englishmen to live in Natal. Compared to most shipwrecked mariners the crew of the *Good Hope* were lucky. Most of the ship's cargo was saved and the survivors bartered copper rings and

beads with the local Bantu for food and ivory. Quite quickly they amassed three tons of ivory.

Even more luckily, among the other things *Good Hope* had been carrying were parts of a ship which was to have been assembled in Cape Town. Under the *Good Hope's* captain, John Adams, the survivors set about assembling the ship in the harbour area. When the ship was built Captain Adams and the majority of the survivors sailed off to Madagascar but five men elected to stay in Natal. In time they were joined by survivors from two other wrecks; they banded together to build a boat using only locally found materials. The completed vessel was sailed to Cape Town in twelve days, so impressing the Governor of the Cape, Simon van der Stel, that he bought her for 400 florins and christened her *Centaur.*

Van der Stel was so intrigued by the stories the survivors told him of Natal's trading possibilities that he decided to purchase the territory for his employers, the Dutch East India Company. He charged a ship's captain called Pieter Jan Timmerman with the task and despatched him for Natal aboard the sailing vessel *Noord* in October, 1689.

When Timmerman arrived in Natal he found a chieftain called Inyangesa and persuaded him to affix his mark to a piece of paper, stating that in return for 1 000 guilders' worth of trade goods — beads, trinkets and iron-mongery — the area around what is today Durban Harbour was henceforth the property of the Dutch East India Company.

With the deed in his possession Captain Timmerman set off for the Cape but was wrecked near Algoa Bay. Timmerman was killed, the bill of sale lost and only four of the 18 men on board his ship made it back to Cape Town. Sixteen years later Captain Johannes Gerbrantzer, a survivor of the original voyage, was sent back to Natal to make good the deal. Gerbrantzer found Inyangesa dead and his son reigning in his place.

Inyangesa's son evidenced only the vaguest notion of written contracts and held the view that contractual obligations were not binding on subsequent generations. Captain Gerbrantzer did not press the issue; he sailed away and the Dutch East India Company's purchase plans were forgotten.

Inyangesa's people disappeared from Natal shortly after Gerbrantzer's visit. They were wiped out by another Nguni clan led by a chieftan called Shadwa. Folklore has it that when Shadwa's people reached what is today Durban, his court jester looked down from a ridge and spied the harbour, inspired by its shape he roared with laughter and said "Behold, *Iteku,*" – the one-testicled thing. To this day the African name for Durban, *eTekwini*, derives from the jester's remark.

After the Dutch East India Company's failed attempt to purchase it, history virtually ignores Natal for more than a hundred years. By then, in the early nineteenth century, the British were ensconced at the Cape, having driven out the Dutch. In 1822 two former British naval officers, Lieutenant Francis

George Farewell and Lieutenant James Saunders King, were engaged in the time-honoured pursuit of seeking their fortunes and decided to see if that goal could be achieved by founding an ivory trading settlement in Natal.

Lieut. Francis George Farewell, one of the first permanent White settlers in Natal. (Cape Archives)

In 1823 aboard their ships the *Salisbury* and the *Julia* they were caught in a severe storm off the Natal coast and sought shelter on the lee side of a high headland. They discovered there what they took to be a river mouth fronted by a sand bar. The smaller of the ships, the *Julia*, sailed over the obstruction and to Lieutenant Farewell's joyful incredulity he found himself in a safe harbour – the same harbour that the Dutch had wanted to buy in the previous century.

The men decided that "Port Natal", as they named it, was the ideal spot for their settlement and by April of the following year an advance party under the nominal leadership of one Harry Francis Fynn had arrived at the harbour and started building shelters. At first there was no sign at all of the other Natal settlers, the Nguni-speaking Bantu, but after a few days one or two frightened tribesmen emerged from the bush and Fynn learned something of recent Nguni history. A great leader called Shaka had arisen to the north. He was chief of a people called the Zulus and controlled a mighty army which wreaked devastation wherever it struck.

Incredible as it may appear, it seems that the British were partially responsible for the founding of the Zulu nation. In 1807 the Acting Governor of the Cape had despatched 21 men under the command of a military surgeon, Robert Cowan, to cross overland from the Cape to Delagoa Bay. The men were never seen again. No-one knows what happened but it seems that by the time Cowan reached what is today Zululand he was the only survivor.

Somewhere in Zululand Cowan met a Nguni exile who was travelling under the alias Dingiswayo – 'the troubled one'. Dingiswayo's real name was Godongwana and he had fled from his own Mtetwa people after failing in an attempt to kill the ruling chief. By the time he met Cowan, Dingiswayo had discovered that the old chief was dead and decided it was time to go home. Cowan's route and his coincided so Dingiswayo agreed to guide the White man.

No-one knows what sort of relationship formed between the two but it certainly was a momentous one. Somewhere on the journey Cowan died and Dingiswayo inherited his horse and gun. Both these items were completely unknown among the Nguni clans in Natal at the time and so when Dingiswayo arrived home he had no trouble at all in convincing his people that he should be their ruler.

What he did then has to have been a result of an exchange of ideas with Cowan. Like other Nguni leaders, Dingiswayo consolidated his power by conquering neighbouring clans but whereas normal practice at the time was then to eliminate them, Dingiswayo allowed the clans to live in peace as long as they paid him allegiance. He strengthened these alliances by embarking on a series of dynastic marriages which bonded the clan rulers to him by family ties.

Dingiswayo was unique among Nguni leaders at the time in ruling benignly and altruistically by political amalgamation rather than extermination. Even more indicative of Cowan's influence, Dingiswayo made strenuous efforts to establish trade with the Portuguese at Delagoa Bay and even tried to form a factory system for preparing hides in his village kraals. Sadly the Portuguese responded to this initiative with complete indifference.

At this time the Zulus were a small, insignificant clan who lived on the banks of the White Umfolozi River, south-east of Dingiswayo's domain. Some time before Dingiswayo took power the Mtetwa had given refuge to a young Zulu boy and his mother. The woman had given birth to an illegitimate son by the chief of one of the Zulu clans and she and her son, Shaka, had been driven into exile.

When Dingiswayo took power he noticed that Shaka showed extraordinary promise as a warrior. In fact Shaka singlehandedly transformed the face of warfare among his people. At the time the chief weapon was a light throwing assegai. Shaka devised a new stabbing assegai with a heavy, broad blade and a short stout shaft, something very similar to a short sword.

Although the Nguni already used shields, it took Shaka to turn the shield into an offensive weapon. He taught his warriors to hook the edge of their shield over the edge of their opponent's shield in such a way that the man's flank was exposed. It was then an easy matter to sink the stabbing assegai deep into the man's body. Shaka soon proved his new weapons in battle and Dingiswayo began to see in him not only a fine warrior but a future leader of the Zulus, one who would strengthen his people to the point where they might serve as a buffer for the Mtwetwa against the more powerful clans to the north.

When the old Zulu king died, Shaka descended on the Zulu royal kraal with an escort of warriors and simply took over, killing the rightful successor to the throne. He then proceeded to do for military tactics what he had done for weaponry. Before Shaka came along Nguni warfare consisted of two groups charging each other pell-mell and then retreating hastily. Shaka taught his troops the value of discipline and tactics. He divided his soldiers into four groups: one group, 'the chest', closed with the enemy at the outset of the battle while two other groups formed 'horns' and charged round on either side of the main group to encircle them. The fourth unit consisted of reinforcements called 'loins' who were reserves and who sat with their backs to the action to avoid getting excited until they were needed.

Shaka's leadership turned the Zulus into a powerful force who quickly quadrupled the size of their territory. But Shaka, unlike Dingiswayo, was not a benign ruler. His empire was maintained by force of arms and he had no clear goals beyond conquest so he killed and conquered without respite in a reign of terror which sent other tribal groups fleeing for their lives.

When Fynn's advance party arrived in Natal the land around the natural harbour was virtually empty because Shaka had driven all the clans into hiding or permanent exile. When Fynn learned that Natal was Shaka's personal property he decided to go and see him. Contact was made with the Zulus and Shaka granted Fynn and Lieutenant Farewell – who had timeously arrived at Port Natal – an audience.

When the men arrived at Shaka's royal kraal they were stunned by the size of his army and the discipline of his troops. They were also stunned by Shaka, who during the audience, kept casually flicking his hand to indicate that he wished this or that member of his entourage immediately executed, the sentence being carried out as the visitors watched.

Shaka liked his White visitors and on a subsequent visit Farewell persuaded him to sign a document granting him title to Port Natal and 3 500 square miles of surrounding territory. Of course Shaka had no intention of taking the document seriously and was later to sign similar documents deeding virtually the same areas of land to two other visitors. Nonetheless Farewell was very pleased and returned to Port Natal in high good humour. On 27th August, 1824 he hoisted the Union Jack near the harbour and declared Port Natal a British outpost.

The settlers soon found that the wealth of ivory they had hoped to tap did not exist. They had been relying on the Zulus to bring in the ivory but elephant hunting with assegais was dangerous to the point of lunacy and so very little hunting took place. Before long disillusionment set in and most of the original settler group returned to Cape Town. Six remained and their names must be recorded because they were the true founders of the Natal we know today. They were Joseph Powell; Thomas Halstead; Harry Francis Fynn; Henry Ogle; John Cane and Lieutenant

Farewell. Two years later these men were joined by Farewell's partner, Lieutenant King, and a young man called Nathaniel Isaacs. King brought with him Farewell's wife Elizabeth who became the first White woman to live permanently in Natal.

The early days of the settlement were very hard. Indeed when Elizabeth Farewell arrived the men were embarrassed to greet her because the rags they wore barely covered their bodies, yet somehow the settlement survived. It can only have done so because of the daring and adventurous nature of the founders. Although they all purported to be men of trade they were in fact adventurers with the restless natures which take men to dangerous, exciting places for nothing more than the thrill of the unknown. It is worth pausing for just a moment to consider the destinies of these eight men.

Isaacs became a close friend of Shaka and at the age of 18 was placed in command of a Zulu army of 5 000 men and sent to make war on a particularly stubborn enemy. He won. At the age of 23 he tired of Natal and sailed away never to return. He started a trading company in England but was unable to settle down and moved to West Africa where for many years he lived alone on a plantation in Sierra Leone.

Thomas Halstead, who proved to be mentally deficient, nonetheless died a hero's death. Shaka's successor Dingane lured a famous Voortrekker leader called Piet Retief and 70 others, including Halstead, to his royal kraal. Choosing a moment when they were unarmed and unsuspecting Dingane ordered them killed. Before he died Halstead killed two Zulus.

John Cane was killed soon after when he joined a force which attacked the Zulus as a reprisal for Retief's death.

Joseph Powell disappeared in 1824 while attempting to reach Portuguese territory overland.

Francis Farewell was murdered in his sleep by an enemy of the Zulus. His partner James King sickened and died in 1828 and was buried in the settlement. Henry Ogle married a Zulu princess and was appointed a Zulu chief.

Fynn left Natal in 1834 but later returned to serve as a magistrate in the town he had helped found.

On 22nd September, 1828 Shaka was assassinated by his half-brother Dingane who then assumed the throne. At the time Shaka's death was greeted with relief but Dingane was to prove by far the worse tyrant; he was moreover deeply suspicious of the White settlers, fearing that they would eventually threaten his kingdom. Dingane had some basis for his fear because the community at Natal was growing.

In 1834 twenty one men and women arrived and at one fell swoop almost doubled the population. They were Boers, the ancestors of South Africa's Afrikaner people, farmers of Dutch origin who had trekked in ox-wagons from the Cape Colony to explore the lands to the north. They were the first emmisaries of what turned into the Great Trek when 14 000 people left the Cape to seek new homes in South Africa's interior.

A number of these trekkers found their way into Natal by crossing the Drakensberg mountains. It is a measure of their determination that to get their ox-wagons over the mountains they dismantled them, carried them over the peaks piece by piece and reassembled them on the other side.

In 1835 there were still fewer than 50 settlers in Port Natal when they gathered together and decided to lay out a proper township which was to be named D'Urban in honour of the Governor of the Cape Colony, Sir Benjamin D'Urban. Almost immediately the apostrophe was dropped and D'Urban became Durban.

Laying out a town showed that the settlers were serious in their intentions to stay in Natal but they lived constantly on the edge of disaster. The Zulus were the true masters of Natal and the settlers' relationship with them was rapidly deteriorating, to the point where Dingane even threatened to attack Durban in 1836. The British, to whom the settlers looked for protection, made it clear that they considered Natal Zulu territory where the settlers lived on Dingane's sufferance.

It was in this atmosphere that Piet Retief, a Boer trek leader, arrived at Durban and proposed making common cause with the settlers. They eagerly accepted and Retief went off to see Dingane to win permission for the Boers to settle in Natal. Dingane was very suspicious of Retief and almost immediately made plans to kill him.

On 4th February, 1838 Dingane put his mark on a document granting the Boers large tracts of land and then invited them to a feast and dance. When the dance was at its height the frenzied warriors launched themselves at the unarmed White men and killed them all. A few hours later Dingane sent out three regiments of warriors to attack the remaining Boers who were camped in some disorder waiting for Retief to return.

The Zulus attacked just before dawn and killed 41 men, 56 women, 185 children and some 250 Hottentot servants. The town which grew up on the site of this massacre is today called Weenen which means "weeping" in Afrikaans. Shocked and disorganised, the Boers did their best to strike back. A force of 350 Boers attacked the Zulus but were defeated and fled; they have gone down in South African history as the *Vlug Kommando* – 'the commando that ran away'.

The Durban settlers fared no better in their attempts at retribution. 16 of them led a force of 800 natives against the Zulus and 600 of the natives and all but four of the Europeans died on the field. Dingane then made good his threat to attack Durban. The Whites fled to the safety of a ship anchored in the bay while the Zulus ransacked the settlement and killed any natives they could find.

Not surprisingly, after this, many of the settlers abandoned Durban and sailed for Cape Town. Truth to tell they were not giving up very much, as Durban consisted of little more than a few haphazardly built shacks planted in the sand. However, Voortrekkers continued to arrive in Natal, carried by the impetus of the Great Trek, and they determined to stay in spite of the Zulu threat. In May, 1838 they annexed the settlement and declared it the independant Republic of Natalia.

One of the chief reasons the Boers left the Cape was

Dingane's kraal Umgungundlovu ('the secret plot of the elephant'), from Gardiner's *Journey to the Zulu Country* (1836). (Cape Archives)

to get away from the British but it seemed to be their fate that the English would follow them wherever they went. No sooner had the Boers claimed Natal than the British arrived and formally took possession of it for Great Britain. The British did so because they were concerned about reports that the Boers were planning to attack the Zulus and because they believed that British subjects living in Durban were in danger from Dingane. They felt to some extent responsible for the actions of the Boers whom they regarded as British subjects by virtue of their former residence in the Cape, a British colony, and they felt it was their duty to take some responsibility for controlling Boer actions. Occupying Durban and imposing British authority there seemed to be the best way of ensuring that peace was kept.

The Boers heard the news as they made ready to attack the Zulus and decided to ignore the new regime until after they had attended to the business at hand. In a solemn ceremony they made a vow that they would avenge those killed by Dingane. One week later, on 16th December, 16, 1838 they were given the opportunity to do so. They crossed into Zululand, chose a position of exceptional strength and waited for the Zulus to attack. The Zulus did so at first light and discovered to their cost that the Boers, who had formed their ox-wagons into a defensive circle or laager and were well-armed, were a formidable enemy. More

than 3 000 Zulu warriors died that day but not one Boer was killed. The battle was fought on the banks of a river and it is said that the waters ran red with Zulu blood. Ever since that day the river has been called Blood River.

Cheered by their decisive victory the Boers flooded down into central Natal, established farms there and founded a capital for their Republic on a site some 80 kilometres inland from Durban. They called the town Pietermaritzburg and to this day it remains Natal's capital city. Everything seemed to be in the trekkers' favour because, barely a year after occupying it, the British quit Durban and the Voortrekker flag was hoisted there once again.

As soon as the British left the Boers turned once more to the problem of the Zulus. There would never be peace in Natal while Dingane remained on the Zulu throne so they determined to remove the threat once and for all by force of arms. A strong force comprised of Boers and dissident Zulus drove Dingane from Zululand. Shortly thereafter Dingane was killed and a pliant Zulu chieftan called Mpande proclaimed the new Zulu king.

Everything pointed to a prosperous future for the Boer Republic but on their return from Zululand the victorious Boers took with them 36 000 head of cattle and, very unwisely, more than 1 000 'orphaned' Zulu 'apprentices' who were forced into domestic service.

The Battle of Blood River, from a drawing by Charles Peers. On 16th December, 1838, Andries Pretorius and his Voortrekkers defeated Dingane, the Zulu chief, thus avenging the murder of Piet Retief and his companions at a conference in Dingane's camp the previous February. (Cape Archives)

The British, who at this time were fighting against slavery and to whom the taking of 'apprentices' seemed to be very nearly the same thing, were alarmed at the action and issued an order to the Governor of the Cape to re-occupy Durban.

The order might have been rescinded if the Boers had acted diplomatically but instead they made matters worse by attacking local African tribes who had returned to their traditional lands on hearing of Dingane's death. These lands were the same ones that the Boers were turning into farms and they had no intention of giving them up so the Africans were driven out.

When news of these events reached Cape Town the governor of the Cape had no choice but to order the nearest British garrison to occupy Durban immediately. The job fell to Captain Thomas Charlton Smith, who had been commander of a small fort 240 kilometres south of Durban. With 263 men and 250 servants and their dependants and 60 oxwagons he set off in an arduous journey northward which included crossing 122 rivers.

When he finally arrived in Durban on 4th May, 1842, Smith found the Boers prepared to fight to prevent a British occupation. After some initial fruitless parlaying Smith attacked, only to be soundly defeated and beaten back to Durban's little fort which the Boers promptly besieged.

Smith's situation was desperate: more than 500 people were crammed into the earthen stockade with limited food and water. His only hope was to send for reinforcements but the Boers had guards everywhere. The British chanced everything on the loyalty and bravery of a 29-year-old Natalian called Dick King who had distinguished himself in action against the Zulus four years previously.

King was asked to ride to Grahamstown, more than 900 kilometres south, to seek help, a journey which usually took three weeks. King rode there in ten days – actually in eight, because for two days he lay flat on his back with fever. Reinforcements were immediately despatched to Durban and the siege was broken 34 days after it had begun, by which time Smith's men were down to quarter rations.

All hopes for a Boer republic in Natal were now dashed. In 1843 Queen Victoria formally announced that Natal was to become one of her colonies and in due course the British government decided that the territory should be administered as an extension of the Cape Colony. The news was received predictably by the Boers, many of whom decided to leave Natal for either the Transvaal or the Orange Free State, Boer republics where the meddling British hand had, as yet, not been felt.

The number of Boer families in Natal rapidly dwindled from more than 400 to less than 100 while at the same time the number of blacks jumped dramatically as those displaced by Dingane returned home. In 1846 there were some 40 000 blacks to only 3 000 whites in Natal and the imbalance grew ever more extreme.

By the mid 1850s the number of blacks had increased to 150 000 and the British were seriously concerned that, unless they could substantially increase the number of Whites living there, Natal would never be a functioning colony. They took immediate steps to encourage the immigration of British farmers, tradesmen and merchants and, partly because conditions in England were pretty grim at this time, the immigrants flooded in. Between 1848 and 1851 more than 3 000 Britons arrived in Natal, spurred on by misleading tales of a settled, prosperous colony.

When they arrived at Durban harbour they were sadly disillusioned. Near-nude Africans carried shocked English women ashore on to a sandy beach dotted with rude huts. Most of the immigrants were housed in tents until they constructed their own wattle and mud dwellings; their nights were often interrupted by the lions, hyenas and elephants which roamed on the edge of the settlement and to walk near a river was foolhardy because of the crocodiles which brazenly hunted on the banks.

Stranded thousands of kilometres from home there was little the settlers could do except to try and improve their lot and this they quickly did, spreading out to form settlements at Richmond, named after the English seat of the Duke of Buccleuch, and Verulam, named for the English Earl of Verulam. Pietermaritzburg literally bulged with people as many of the immigrants were attracted to what was then the most bustling town in Natal but Durban too thrived as a port and trading centre.

In 1854 Durban formed its first town council and in 1860 the first railway in South Africa was opened with a station in Durban and another on Durban Point.

The fertile well-watered Natal coastal strip was discovered to be ideal for sugar cane production and by 1860 Natal was exporting sugar to England. The Zulus had no taste for work in the sugar cane fields and there were not enough Whites to do the work so a solution was found in the importation of indentured labourers from India. Thus it was that in 1860 the first shipload of Asians arrived at the port, the founders of a community which is today half a million strong.

The British were now firmly in control of Natal and while Mpande lived their policy towards the Zulus was one of benign neglect. Under Mpande's peaceful rule the Zulus recovered from the blows they had suffered at the hands of the Boers and became even stronger than they were in Dingane's day. Mpande achieved a feat almost unheard of in early Zulu history, he died peacefully of old age.

Cetshwayo, who succeeded Mpande, was an intelligent, forceful man but the times were against him. The British were established to his south and the Boers to the west. The Boers wanted more land while powerful elements in Britain were coming to believe that to allow the existence of a number of separate entities within greater South Africa was impractical; administratively difficult and a constant drain on the British exchequer. The answer, they believed, was to unite all the territories in one political confederation. In 1877 Sir Bartle Frere was appointed Governor of the Cape with a mandate to achieve this.

In order to render federation feasible something had to be done about the Zulus whose territory marched

Cetshwayo, chief of the Zulus, was forced into the last Zulu war by an ultimatum from the British, who hoped to unite all the territories in South Africa into one political confederation. (Cape Archives)

side by side with Natal's for hundreds of kilometres. While the Zulus remained uncontrolled they posed a constant threat to British lives. Their power would have to be broken and war was deliberately chosen as the means to do it. An ultimatum was delivered to the Zulu throne demanding, among other things, the disbanding of the Zulu army. Cetshwayo could not accede to the demands, which amounted in effect to asking him to surrender his sovereignty, and so in early January, 1879, Lord Frederic Chelmsford, in command of 16 800 men, attacked Zululand.

The British soldiers were well armed and well supplied and they took the field against an enemy armed only with shields and spears, so they viewed the undertaking not so much as a war but as a routine military exercise. In so thinking they made a mistake which was to cost the lives of thousands of British soldiers. The Zulu nation was about to inflict upon the British one of the most stunning defeats in their history.

Chelmsford ordered a central column of his men to make their base at Isandhlwana mountain, about 16 kilometres inside Zululand. Presumably because they so seriously underestimated their enemy, the British neglected either to form their wagons into a protective laager, or to fortify their camp. At approximately 11.45 on the morning of 22nd January, 1879, 20 000 Zulu warriors attacked and the British were overwhelmed. 1 329 British officers and men were killed in a staggering defeat.

Britain was stunned when news of the defeat was announced, not only because of the military implications but because of the savagery of the victors: a drummer boy caught among the wagons was nailed

upside down and his throat slit; fleeing British soldiers were hunted down and disembowelled. Zulu custom dictated that the warriors should do this to release the dead man's spirit but to the British, unfamiliar with Zulu customs, the story was horrifying. Of the entire British column only 55 White men survived. The Zulus for their part may have won the battle but they lost 3 000 men in doing so and Cetshwayo mourned the losses as "a spear thrust in the side of the nation".

Even as the Zulus mopped up at Isandhlwana, a second Zulu force moved towards another target, an unfortified mission station at Rorke's Drift just inside Natal which the British were using as a field hospital. When warning was received that at least 4 000 Zulus were on their way to the station there were only 350 British troops within the compound and they were completely unprepared to withstand an attack. Their commanding officer, Lieutenant John Chard of the Royal Engineers, thought momentarily of fleeing but then decided the better chance of survival lay in standing to fight.

When the Zulu forces were spotted "black as hell and thick as grass," as one of the defenders, army chaplain George Smith, put it, the prospect proved too much for some of the troops who broke and ran. Within minutes only 140 men remained at the station and some 20 of those were either hospital patients or men otherwise incapable of fighting. Wave after wave of Zulus flung themselves at the mission and each time Chard and his men repelled them.

The Zulu attack began in the late afternoon and continued until dawn. The defenders fired more than 20 000 rounds of ammunition; 17 of them were killed and seven others severely wounded but they held out. Just before dawn the Zulu attacks slackened and Chard and his men, who could barely have survived another rush, peered out to see the warriors withdrawing. Zulu losses were never accurately counted but were at least 500. The Victoria Cross, Britain's highest award for valour, was awarded to 11 of the defenders, the largest number ever given for a single action.

The immediate effect of the Zulu victory at Isandhlwana was to stall the war effort completely until more troops arrived from Britain. If the Zulu army had descended on Natal directly after the battle they would have found the territory almost entirely unprotected but the Zulu army was tired and retired to lick its wounds. Only in March did significant battles begin again.

On 12th March, 1879, a British force escorting a wagon train was surprised at the Intombi River and the commanding officer and 79 men were killed. Later that same month, on 28th March, a British force attempting to storm a Zulu stronghold at Hlobane lost 15 officers and 79 men.

However, on the following day the British won a very significant victory. The full force of the Zulu army, 20 000 strong, attacked a British position at Kambula, defended by 2 086 men – a situation very similar to the one which had prevailed at Isandhlwana. Yet this time the British easily withstood the attack and beat off the Zulus, inflicting heavy losses. The difference was that the British had stopped underestimating their enemy and were commanded by a very fine officer, Sir Henry Evelyn Wood, V.C. Wood chose his defensive position well and deployed his troops and their weapons effectively. After this defeat Cetshwayo and his advisers realised that bravery was not enough to withstand the might of the British empire but it was too late to turn back, the tragedy of the Zulu people had to unfold to its bitter end.

On the face of it the British position was still serious. 1 300 men were besieged at a former mission station in Eshowe and Chelmsford was unable to relieve them, but Britain was pouring in reinforcements and it was even then only a matter of time before the Zulus were defeated. On 29th March Lord Chelmsford personally led a relief column towards the beleaguered garrison. On 2nd April when the column had reached Gingindlovu, 10 000 Zulus attacked but 1 200 fell under withering fire and the attackers withdrew.

Eshowe was relieved the next day and Chelmsford, sure of victory, was free to launch a final attack on the Zulus. It was three months in the planning, but while Chelmsford was making his preparations the Zulus struck another blow which was to be felt around the world.

On 31st March His Highness Louis Napoleon, the Prince Imperial of France, arrived at Durban, having won permission from the British to witness the fighting but not to take part in it. On 1st June, 1879 the Prince Imperial rode out on a routine patrol with eight other men. At four that afternoon the patrol was surprised by some 40 Zulu warriors who attacked and killed the prince and two troopers.

Louis had been popular in England where he lived in exile from Republican France and he was a person of political importance, the only person who could have restored the Napoleonic dynasty to his country. Now he was dead and his cause lost. The French blamed the British for his death and such was the anti-British sentiment that for a while it was unsafe for an Englishman to appear on a French street.

In Natal the British advance continued inexorably towards the Zulus' destruction. On 4th June, 1879, the last battle of the Zulu war was fought at Ulundi. More than 500 British troops formed into a tight square while 20 000 Zulus surrounded the British and attacked from all sides, but they were unable to get within 30 metres of the British troops. In 45 minutes the battle ended with 12 British dead and 1 500 Zulus killed. Cetshwayo watched the action from a nearby hill and when he realised that his troops had lost he fled.

The war was over. Cetshwayo was captured two months later and exiled first to Cape Town and then to England. His country was partitioned into 13 districts, each ruled by a British-appointed chief. A

Dabulamanzi and John Robert Dunn (1833–1895). Dunn, a pioneer, trader, big game hunter and one-time confidant of Cetshwayo, was appointed a White chief over the Zulus after the Zulu War. His descendants still live in the area he once ruled. (Cape Archives)

White man, John Dunn, who had once been a confidant of Cetshwayo, was given the largest tract of land and he ruled it as a personal fiefdom, marrying a string of Zulu wives whom he selected by reconnoitring river banks where the local maidens gathered to bathe. John Dunn's descendants still live in part of the area he once ruled and have become a social group distinct from both Zulus and Whites.

It sometimes seems that Natal's history is a series of battles punctuated by brief periods of peace. Already the factors causing the next war were in operation. In 1877, as part of the confederation plan, Britain had annexed the Transvaal. To many Boers it was yet another example of the refusal of the British to allow them to live unfettered. Discontent mounted steadily until in December, 1880 the Boers resolved to fight for their independence.

On 20th December hostilities commenced and once more Natal was embroiled in a bitter battle. General Sir George Colley, the Lieutenant Governor of Natal, felt it his duty to relieve the British loyalists who were beleaguered in various Transvaal towns and at once mustered 1 000 men to go to their aid. Before they could set out, however, the Boers brought the war to Natal by invading the colony and lying in wait for the British at Laing's Neck.

The British had underestimated the Zulus and now they repeated the mistake with the Boers. In the first engagement on 28th January, 1881, General Colley lost 73 men and had a hundred wounded. The Boers suffered hardly any casualties. Colley fared no better in the next battle when the British were forced to take refuge on a plateau of the Ingogo Heights which was unsuitable for defence. 150 British soldiers died for the loss of eight Boers.

Colley, no doubt smarting from his double defeat, decided to mount an expedition which would save his reputation. In the early hours of 27th February, 1881, he and a large force occupied Majuba mountain near the Boer positions. The next morning the Boers were astounded to discover the mountain occupied but bravely stormed the British positions and their excellent marksmanship, aided by the easily-visible red British uniforms, gained them victory. 92 British were killed, including Colley, and another 134 were wounded. The Boer forces lost only one man.

After this defeat the British restored complete self-government to the Transvaal, subject only to the proviso that the Boers acknowledged British suzerainty. It was clear that the Boers had won a total victory.

The outcome of the war was a great shock to Natal, not least because Natalians had been so deeply involved in the annexation of the Transvaal: one of Natal's distinguished figures, Sir Theophilus Shepstone, had proclaimed the annexation and Natalians held important posts in the Republic. For a time there was open discontent in Natal at what seemed to be a lack of will on the part of the British but soon the war was forgotten as peace once more allowed the development of Natal to proceed.

Immigrants poured in and slowly the comforts of civilisation found their way to the colony. Piped water

was installed in Pietermaritzburg, the railway line was extended until Durban and the Transvaal were linked, and engineers wrestled successfully with the difficult problem of increasing the depth of water over the sand bar which blocked Durban's harbour. By 1887 the population of Natal numbered nearly half a million, of which 35 866 were White, 32 312 were Indian and 408 922 were Black.

The rapid growth of the Indian population and their success as businessmen alarmed White colonists who brought pressure to bear on the British government to prevent further Asian immigration to Natal. The influx of immigrants, White and Asian, created land pressure which was alleviated somewhat when Zululand and Tongaland, even further north, were added to Natal's territory in 1897 and White farmers moved into these areas.

The influx of Whites into Zululand created problems for the local inhabitants who had a growing population and shrinking lands on which to put them. Sadly, apart from apportioning totally inadequate amounts of land for Bantu reserves, there was no real attempt to deal with the problem which has persisted to the present day.

As time went by the colonists began to identify with Natal rather than with England. As this feeling grew, so did demands for a measure of self-government and in 1893 the British allowed Natal to adopt responsibility for making its own laws.

One of the first things the new government did was to try and take away the vote from the Indian population, a move which appalled a visiting Indian lawyer called Mohandas Karamchand Ghandi. Ghandi resolved to fight for Indian rights and settled in Natal where he opened a law practice. It was in Natal that he formed the strategy known as passive resistance which he was later to use in India with devastating effect on the British. Non-violent resistance, embodying the principle that one should hate oppression but love the oppressor, was a philosophy nurtured under the Natal sky.

Ghandi went on to lead the Indian people to independence and is one of the most famous men ever to have lived in Natal but the treatment he received in Natal casts no glory on the White settlers of the period. Once when he returned from a visit to India in 1897, Whites attacked him and he was forced to flee disguised as an Indian policeman. On another occasion he evidenced interest in attending an Anglican church service but the vicar was so afraid of the reaction of his White congregation that he asked Ghandi to sit outside and listen to the service.

It must be said that Ghandi's best efforts were to no avail in Natal – the Indians were duly disenfranchised and further Asian immigration stopped.

The century drew to a close and as it did so war broke out again. In 1884 gold had been discovered in the Transvaal in quantities hitherto undreamed of anywhere in the world. The resulting gold rush led to a flood of non-Boers into the Transvaal and, ever-fearful of losing their cherished independence, the Boer government refused them voting rights, causing much dissatisfaction among them.

As most of these *Uitlanders,* as the non-Boers were called, were British, they addressed their complaints to the British government which brought pressure to bear on the Transvaal to redress the grievances. The Transvaal's leader, President Paul Kruger refused, however, to grant the *uitlanders* the rights they sought. This alone would not have been enough to cause a war, but the discovery of gold had given President Kruger the finance with which to further a cherished dream, the throwing off of all ties with Britain, even the light suzerainty ties he had agreed to after Majuba, and the creation of a Boer dominion in South Africa.

The British were alarmed at the obvious military preparations of the Boers and relations between the two countries deteriorated rapidly until on 2nd October, 1899, the Transvaal declared war with Great Britain. Once again Natal was to be wrenched from peace to bloodshed.

This war, the Boer War, as it came to be called, was the first modern war. It introduced to the world the delights of machine guns, mobile artillery, barbed-wire-fronted trenches and concentration camps. At the same time it was the last gentleman's war. At one point when a Boer general besieging a British-occupied town ran out of medicine for his troops who had contracted dysentery, he applied to the British commander for assistance. The Briton not only sent out the necessary medication but added to it some brandy from his own private stock. The Boers were equally civilised, and habitually refrained from shelling besieged towns on a Sunday because it was the Lord's day.

The Boers invaded Natal on 12th October, 1899. They quickly advanced to Newcastle and then on to Dundee where in a fierce action they were initially repelled but caused such heavy losses that British forces evacuated the town a few days later. The Boers' main force of some 20 000 men then advanced on Ladysmith and between 29th October and 2nd November managed to surround and besiege the town.

Some historians argue that if the Boers had left a small force to keep up the siege and had struck towards the coast the whole course of South African history could have been changed. The British were outnumbered by the Boers at this point in the war and if the Boer forces had taken Pietermaritzburg and then Durban, gaining access to the sea and a safe harbour for supplies to reach them, it might have proved impossible for the British to dislodge them. In the event, the Boers decided not to proceed until Ladysmith had fallen and the stubborn refusal of the town to submit gave the British time to flood Natal with reinforcements.

In November, under pressure from his subordinates, notably the Natal-born Louis Botha, who was to prove one of the most able Boer leaders during the war and for whom greater glory lay waiting, the Boer general, Piet Joubert, at last agreed to let a portion of his men move south from Ladysmith. On 15th November, near Colenso, these men ambushed a British military train, wrecking it and capturing 70 prisoners, including a young war correspondent from England called Winston Churchill, later to become one of Britain's most famous Prime Ministers. Churchill subsequently

escaped and his exploits in South Africa made him famous for the first time.

By December, 1899 the Boer forces had made great gains: they had conquered the Cape midlands, much of the northern Cape and northern Natal and their forces besieged Ladysmith, Mafikeng and Kimberley. In the week ending 16th December 1899 the British tried to raise the sieges of Kimberley and Ladysmith but failed so dismally that the week goes down in British history as Black Week.

Within a few days of each other the British forces were soundly defeated at three different points by the Boers who showed themselves not only to be brave soldiers but sound strategists. Black Week saw the death of 3 000 British soldiers, the worst losses coming in Natal when Sir Redvers Buller failed in a bid to relieve Ladysmith by forcing his way across the Tugela River at Colenso. 1 127 of his men died in the attempt.

After these defeats the flaws in Britain's military machine became glaringly obvious to other major European powers. This had severe political repercussions, particularly in Germany, a country with whom British relations were already so strained that the war which was to follow 14 years later even then seemed likely. Britain's response to the three defeats was to mount an enormous and determined effort to crush the Boers by force of numbers. 200 000 men were readied for South Africa and England's most famous living soldier, Field Marshall Lord Roberts, was placed in command. Lord Kitchener of Khartoum, then one of the most lauded men in England, was named as second-in-command.

Roberts arrived at Cape Town on 10th January, 1900 and at the head of a vast army began marching north. Kimberley was relieved on 19th February, and Roberts moved on towards Bloemfontein, the capital of the Orange Free State.

Meanwhile, in Natal, Ladysmith was still under siege and Sir Redvers Buller was still trying to relieve it. His second attempt ended in disaster when his forces were driven off a hill called Spioenkop for the loss of 1 200 men.

Conditions within the besieged town were deteriorating. 2 000 people lay suffering from dysentery in a hospital meant for 200, food was in such short supply that eggs fetched 48/- a dozen, the staple diet was horse meat and upwards of 70 people were dying each week of disease, but the British had no intention of surrendering.

On 5th February Buller tried again and was again repulsed, this time for the loss of 400 men. A fourth attempt finally won through on 27th February, 1900. The British commander of the army in the town, Sir George White, met the troops with the words "I thank God we have kept the flag flying."

Once Ladysmith was relieved the tide of battle in Natal, as in the rest of South Africa, turned, and from then on it was the Boer forces who came under severe pressure. A wary British public only truly believed it when Mafikeng was relieved on 18th May. By 11th June the whole of Natal was once more in British hands; the Transvaal capital, Pretoria, had been captured and President Kruger had fled to Holland.

A Boer campsite during the Boer War. The boy standing in the centre of the photograph looks remarkably young. (Cape Archives)

The British thought the war was over but they reckoned without the stubbornness of the Boers who for more than a year kept harrying the British in commando actions. In October, 1901 the Boers even made another attempt to invade Natal but were stopped at Mount Itala with heavy loss of life.

The latter part of the war was a bitter affair in which the Boers adopted guerilla tactics of banding together in small groups, harrying the British and then melting away into the veld. Faced with a situation in which the guerillas' wives and children, scattered on farms across the country, kept their menfolk well supplied, the British rounded them all up and placed them in the world's first concentration camps, one of which was in Natal.

The war finally ended on 31st May 1902 after 22 000 British and an unknown number of Boers had died. In victory Britain was generous to the defeated Boers and self-government was promised to the newly acquired colonies of Transvaal and the Orange Free State. For Natal victory meant the acquisition of some 12 000 kilometres of additional territory in the north, the districts of Vryheid, Utrecht and part of Wakkerstroom.

For Natal's civilian population the Boer war had caused relatively little hardship. Durban was crammed with refugees, the population almost doubling between 1898 and 1901 from 39 000 to 60 000, but the loss of lucrative markets inland was made up for by the new markets provided in the shape of British troops.

The declaration of peace meant once more the development of Natal could proceed unchecked and Durban, now decidedly larger and more important than Pietermaritzburg, moved rapidly into the modern era. Electricity arrived and in 1902 an electric tram service was introduced. Gradually the ubiquitous sand was tamed and lawns and gardens established where once there had been massive dunes. Holiday-makers began to find their way to the Natal coast, the founders of what is today a huge tourist industry.

The problems of deepening Durban harbour were finally overcome and in 1904 a ship of nearly 13 000 tons steamed safely through the entrance, finally establishing the viability of Durban as a major port. A sad effect of the rapid civilisation of Natal was the effect on the animal population which was hunted to the point of extinction. Today, were it not for game reserves, there would be no big wild animals left in the province.

As the echoes of the gunfire of the Boer war died away the idea of federation began once more to occupy the thoughts of politicians. After lengthy negotiations the voters of Natal were given the opportunity to choose whether or not to join with the Cape, Orange Free State and Transvaal in a great Union of South Africa. In spite of the memories of the Boer War an overwhelming majority voted in favour of Union and on 31st May, 1910 Natal voluntarily relinquished its status as an independent British colony to become a province of the Union of South Africa. The first Prime Minister was the Natalian Louis Botha who had fought with such distinction for the Boers during the war.

While it is true to say that since joining the Union, Natal has relinquished its centre-stage role in South African politics, economically the province has prospered along with the rest of South Africa. The period from Union until the present day has been marked by a rapid expansion of industry, mining and agriculture. The growth of the economy created a great need for labour and both the Indian and African communities entered the industrial sector, forsaking

their rural lifestyles for urban ones and irrevocably changing the future course of their histories.

Union meant an influx of Afrikaans-speaking South Africans into Natal but in spite of this English is still the most commonly spoken language in the province. The Indian community has adopted English as a home language and the Zulus have adopted it as their second language.

Natal is very proud of its English heritage and her people were enthusiastic supporters of Britain in both World War I and II. During both wars Durban was used as an important British base and Natalians volunteered in large numbers to join the war effort.

After World War II the intense desire of English-speaking Natalians to retain their own identity in a South Africa where Afrikaans-speaking descendants of the Boers were very much in control, led periodically to calls for the province to secede from the Union.

Perhaps the most vigorous manifestation of this sentiment came in 1960 when the South African government proposed that South Africa should cut its last ties with Britain and adopt a republican form of government. White South Africa as a whole voted narrowly in favour of the move but Natal voted overwhelmingly against it. Nonetheless, on 31st May, 1961 Natal became a province of the new Republic of

Londoners gather to hear news of the relief of the siege of Ladysmith. (Cape Archives)

South Africa and in the period since has co-existed well with the other predominantly Afrikaans-speaking provinces, whilst still maintaining a strong English tradition.

Within Natal the imbalance in population which so worried the British a century ago has continued. In 1970 the total population of the province was 2 140 166, of which 444 499 were White, 514 810 were Asian, 66 836 were of mixed race and 1 116 499 were Black. As the Black community began to play an increasing role in the economy of Natal they began to question a system in which they were voteless with very little say in the political life of either their province or of South Africa as a whole. Various political groups were formed to press for change and chief among these organisations was the ANC or African National Congress.

In 1960 the former president general of the ANC, Albert Luthuli, a Zulu, became the first South African to win a Nobel Peace Prize. Luthuli envisaged a future in which South African people of all races exercised political rights in a common legislative body, while the official view of the South African government is that each racial group should determine its own affairs in its own areas. Thus it has created a territory called Kwa-Zulu set aside for the Zulus.

Kwa-Zulu is presently no more than 13 fragmented pieces of land carved out of northern Natal, and the Zulus, led by the charismatic Chief Gatsha Buthelezi, have thus far refused to accept any form of independence for the areas. However, a fledgling Zulu state is once again in existence in traditional Zulu lands and it will without doubt play a significant role in South Africa's future.

The Zulus are the single largest ethnic group in the country and there is a general feeling within Natal that better co-operation and understanding between them and the other racial groups is essential for the continued prosperity of the province. The same feelings apply towards the Indian population but as yet no clear-cut policy to enable these people to participate more fully in the life of South Africa has been formulated.

A side-effect of the South African government's policy of establishing independent areas for different racial groups has been the addition to Natal of an extra piece of territory. When Transkei, which lies to the south of Natal, became independent its territory cut off an area of the Cape called East Griqualand from other areas of the Cape Province. It was decided that the 3 400 square kilometres of prime farming land should be excised from the Cape and given to Natal to which it is closer geographically and to which many of East Griqualand's peoples already had strong ties. East Griqualand became officially part of Natal on April 1, 1978.

Natal remains South Africa's smallest province but population growth has been so great that it is now Southern Africa's most densely populated area – home to some 20% of all South Africans. The area has rushed into the modern world at breathtaking speed. Barely one hundred years ago Durban was a sandy provisioning spot, and now it is a bustling, modern city with busy streets, an international airport and the busiest harbour in Southern Africa. A second major harbour has been established at Richards Bay in the north, further underlining Natal's economic importance to the rest of South Africa. Progress in the rest of the province has come at a similar pace. In the face of this achievement there can be no doubt that the people of Natal will find a way to face the challenge of the future.

Natal today

Natal is a blessed land, blessed with great beauty, fertile soil, a magnificent coastline, and filled with a rich diversity of people. Natal is the smallest of South Africa's four provinces, covering some 86 967 square kilometres. Geographically it lies on the east coast of South Africa sandwiched between Mozambique to the north and Transkei to the south, stretching inland until it meets the formidable Drakensberg mountain range. The warm Indian Ocean laps against the east coast, and generally the climate is subtropical, giving way to rich grasslands as the land rises to the west.

Geologically Natal is built upon a sandstone base formed millions of years ago as sediments were laid down beneath the sea. About 300 million years ago the earth shifted, pushing the sedimentary sandstone out of the water. For millions of years Natal was a swampy place of heavy rains and humid heat where dinosaurs roamed. Then a huge flood of lava buried the area under a 1 200 metre layer of basalt, which was slowly eroded by heavy rains, leaving the hills and dales which form the Natal we know today.

The eroding process was less effective in the west: today the land slopes steeply downwards from the towering peaks of the Drakensberg, some of which reach 3 600 metres above sea-level, down to the coast some 200 kilometres east. About 300 rivers rush down this steep slope to find their way to the sea at some point along Natal's 480 kilometre length.

So fertile is the land through which they flow and such is the variety of plant life which flourishes in Natal that the province has been called South Africa's Garden Province.

All kinds of people live within Natal's borders. Blacks, Whites and Asians all call themselves Natalians and they have all stamped Natal with their own special marks. The Zulu people once controlled the mightiest empire in Africa and dominated the continent south of the Sahara with their formidable military machine. Then came English rule and there are still many English-speaking Natalians who consider that Natal is their exclusive domain. English is the Province's common language and English habits such as afternoon tea are still practised, and while for the rest of South Africa rugby is the passion, in Natal cricket is the game.

The Asians who live in Natal are descendants of Indian workers brought to Natal to farm the sugar cane plantations more than a century ago. They brought with them Hinduism and Islam, a sharp instinct for trading and a liking for curries to which they have converted many other Natalians.

Natal is South Africa's leading holiday haven. Many vacationers confine themselves to the areas of Durban and the warm and attractive South Coast. Their lack of incentive for further exploration is easy to understand: the sea is always warm, the coast dotted with beautiful bays where privacy can easily be found. Some of South Africa's finest hotels are right on hand and Durban has a vigorous night-life. Why travel further?

Yet Natal has so many other charms to offer: wild animals in game reserves, stunningly beautiful mountains, picturesque drives and seemingly endless stretches of pristine countryside. Just a few kilometres outside Durban it is possible to camp in a deserted spot on the coast, to pluck fish from the ocean and in the evening to gaze up to an unpolluted star-filled sky. A feeling of peace pervades all of Natal yet this sleepy gentle quality is misleading for Natal has a rich history filled with daring adventures and famous battles.

Zululand

Few African words are so instantly recognised as the word Zulu. It conjures up visions of proud, spear-brandishing warriors, of dust raised by the pounding of thousands of feet as the dreaded Zulu war machine sends another wave of men against their red-coated enemies. The British war against the Zulus in the last century ensured the Zulu world-wide fame. The Zulu armed with only spears inflicted crushing defeats on the British who had thought themselves invincible; and Zulu bravery passed into legend.

Quite apart from their fighting prowess the Zulus deserved fame. At the height of their power they controlled an empire so mighty it seemed set to expand its influence indefinintely when the Zulus encountered strange, white-coloured beings who rode upon wild animals and held sticks in their hands which spat death, and their power crumbled.

Zululand was always the heartland of the Zulu people although in their days of greatness they ruled over a much larger area.

The British and the Boers so crushed the Zulus that only now, more than a century later, is a fledgling Zulu state slowly emerging once again. It is called Kwa-Zulu and many problems beset its progress: at the moment it is no more than thirteen fragmented pieces of land within the Zululand borders. There is even debate about whether the creation of a Zulu state is desirable for people who are now largely incorporated into the South African state. Kwa-Zulu's future is hard to predict but it does seem certain that one day the Zulus will once again play a large role in South Africa, sheer numbers guarantee that. They are the single largest ethnic group in the country, numbering more than six million.

Even in their darkest days a Zulu king reigned on a shadowy throne, and today King Goodwill, a descendant of these kings, reigns as a constitutional monarch in Kwa-Zulu. The Zulus uphold their old traditional quite determinedly and they remain deeply respectful to their chiefs and especially to their king. No Zulu stands in his presence and those fortunate enough to be invited to tea with His Majesty are served by women carrying trays while shuffling about on their knees.

Most Zulus firmly believe in the power of their tribal witchdoctors who are still treated with much the same respect and awe that surrounded them when the Zulu nation's power was at its zenith. Then any person 'smelled out' by a witchdoctor as an evil-doer was instantly put to death.

There are two types of witchdoctor: the *Nyanga* or 'doctor' and the *Ngoma* or 'diviner'. The Nyanga treats the sick, often with remarkable success. Ngomas are consulted when somebody has a particular problem, which might be a case of unrequited love or perhaps protection from the evil spells of another witchdoctor. Often the Ngoma divines the troubles by throwing a heap of bones on the ground. The way in which the bones fall tells the witchdoctor what the problem may be.

For a long time modern western thought scoffed at witchdoctors but now a reappraisal is taking place. Some of the Nyanga's traditional remedies are being examined to see whether it is possible that they have information unknown in western medicine, and in some areas witchdoctors are actually being incorporated into the mainstream of medical services with official government backing.

Renewed interest in extra-sensory perception in the west has led to a closer look at the Ngomas too. Witchdoctors undergo a long and arduous apprenticeship and are only allowed to practice when they have passed some fairly difficult tests. For example one Zulu witchdoctor I met was told to find a needle which had been purposely dropped somewhere in the veld by her examiner. She did so in just under seven minutes. The spirits guided her to the place where the needle was lying, she explained.

Another fascinating aspect of Zulu life is their love for beads which they work into intricate necklaces and bracelets. So highly developed has this art become that the Zulus now use beads as a means of communication. For example a love-struck girl will send her man a love-letter made only of beads. Each colour bead has a different meaning. White represents love and purity, black means grief, loneliness or disappointment, green means jealousy, red means tears and longing, yellow represents wealth, pink means poverty, blue means faithfulness while a striped bead implies doubt. These beads can be sewn together in such a way that the lover knows exactly what the message is.

Traditionally Zulu maidens go bare-breasted and in the rural areas of Zululand this undress is the rule. In the really remote areas the girls wear nothing more than a bead girdle to protect their modesty.

Zululand is rich in history and battlefields, the two of which often go together. In the past it also abounded with wild animals, which are today limited to some very fine game reserves. Geographically Zululand is a place of seemingly endless rolling hills. The coastal strip is hot and humid but the inland hills are cooled by the sea breeze and are often covered with misty rain. To the north west Zululand is bordered by Tongaland, to the north by Swaziland and to the east it is separated from the rest of Natal by an ill-defined line which runs just west of Paulpietersburg, Vryheid and Dundee. The main road from Durban skirts the edge of Zululand, following its western and northern boundaries.

The smaller roads which branch off from this main road are often dirt tracks which spend all day winding about, without apparent aim, from one tiny place to another, but frequently they lead to some historically significant spot.

At Umgungundlovu an event took place which is one of the most famous in South African history. The name means 'the secret plot of the elephant' and was the first royal capital of Dingane which he built after treacherously killing his half-brother Shaka. To this kraal in 1837 came a group of Boer voortrekkers under the leadership of Piet Retief, seeking permission to settle in Natal. After signing a document giving them the land they wanted Dingane flicked his fingers and had Retief and his men slaughtered. The Boers took their revenge at the Battle of Blood River which took place just inside the western border of Zululand when they decimated the Zulu warriors. Fearsome in their victory, the Boers descended on Umgungundlovu and razed it to the ground.

Gingindlovu, south of Eshowe, also has a place in Zulu history. Succession to the Zulu throne has been a subject of great confusion because in a polygamous society there are always numerous heirs from different wives, each with his own claim to the throne. In the 1850s, when it became obvious that Mpande was ailing, his heirs began jostling for the right to take-over. In 1856 Cetshwayo, Mpande's eldest son, fought his principal rival, his half brother Mbulazi, at a place called Ndondakusuka. Cetshwayo and his followers not only killed Mbulazi and five other half-brothers but massacred 23 000 of their followers. From that time the site of the battle was known as Mathambo – 'Place of the Bones'. After his victory Cetshwayo built a military stronghold near the battle site which he named Gingindlovu, 'the swallower of the elephant'. The British, incidentally, Anglicized the name to "Gin, gin, I love you".

Rorke's Drift in Zululand is where, during the Zulu war, a handful of British soldiers held off a huge Zulu army and won the most Victoria Crosses ever awarded in a single battle. Isandhlwana is nearby, where in the opening battle of the Zulu war the

The massacre of Piet Retief and his companions on 4th February, 1838, in Dingane's kraal, Umgungundlovu. (Cape Archives)

British were wiped out almost to the last man. Eshowe is another famous name: In January, 1879 a British column was besieged there for ten weeks by the Zulus and the whole of Britain trembled for their fate. Massive reinforcements were required to break the siege and the best the British could do was to abandon the place which was promptly burned to the ground by the Zulus. After the war Eshowe became the capital of Zululand and an important administrative centre.

Today Empangeni is one of Zululand's most important centres. Here in 1905 the first experimental timber plantation was established, the success of which led to extensive timber planting along the whole Zululand coast. Now it is an important railway junction and a centre for sugar, cotton, cattle and timber.

Ulundi, right in the heart of Zululand, is the site of the last battle of the Zulu war. It was then Cetshwayo's royal kraal and when the British attacked on 4th July, 1879, his warriors fought doggedly to defend their king but to no avail. The defeat of the Zulus that day spelt the end of their empire. It is perhaps fitting that Ulundi is the capital of the new Zulu state, Kwa-Zulu. A reconstruction of Cetshwayo's kraal has been erected at Ulundi.

If several places in Zululand have history strongly attached to their names, Richards Bay is a name destined to figure in the history books of the future. South Africa's overseas trade has grown so quickly that great pressure has been placed on the country's existing ports. In 1967 a modern new harbour was opened at Richards Bay to help cope with the increasing volume. A large town is rapidly growing up around the harbour and a number of industries have already been established there. Richards Bay is one of the focal points of development in Natal's future growth and it seems certain that before very long what was once a sleepy village will become a city.

Tongaland

Natal's northernmost portion, Tongaland, is still virtually unknown: few roads cross it and those that do are usually unsurfaced, and there is no major town anywhere within its borders. Tongaland is a flat, sandy, forested place of steamy heat and high rainfall. Bilharzia and crocodile haunt its streams, while tsetse fly and malaria-carrying mosquitos buzz in the air. Not all that long ago this whole area lay below sea level and the soil is still salty, making it difficult to grow crops there.

As if to make up for these deficiencies nature has given Tongaland a wondrous array of forests. Some of the forest trees, such as the wild figs, grow into giants and so dense is their foliage that light seldom penetrates to the forest floor. Nearer the coast the forest thins and gives way to a variety of palms,

among them the lala palm which can easily be tapped to obtain a refreshing drink which also ferments quickly into a strong alcohol.

Tongaland is the home of the Tembe and Mabudu people. They live simply in flimsy huts scattered throughout the 9 000 square kilometres of their land, resisting gently all attempts to bring them into the modern world. Their land borders Swaziland to the west and Mozambique, where many others of their tribe live, to the north.

Nothing much happens in Tongaland, which is the way the locals like it, but in 1898 Tongaland was the scene of one of the most intriguing shipwrecks to take place anywhere on the South African coast. A ship named the *Dorothea* was abandoned at sea eight kilometres off Cape Vidal. A story spread that the ship had been carrying 120 000 ounces of gold which was being smuggled out of South Africa encased in concrete beneath the mast. The wreck was located and numerous attempts were made to salvage the cargo, the only result being that many men lost their lives in the unpredictable waters off the coast. The ship still lies where she foundered and still no-one knows the truth about her mysterious cargo.

The Tongaland coast is wild and desolate and because of the lack of roads can be hard to reach. It is also very dangerous for swimmers because of sharks and treacherous currents. Skilled skin-divers, however, say that the off-shore reefs are so beautiful that they make the risks worthwhile.

Tongaland has some fine lakes, including Lake Sibya which is made up of crystal-clear fresh water which comes from some mysterious unknown source. On the edge of the lake a large number of local tribesmen have been stricken with a mysterious crippling disease called Mseleni disease which no-one can explain. Some scientists have attempted to link the mysterious ailment to the waters of the lake with no success. Mseleni disease remains a medical mystery.

Game reserves

The entire area of Natal was once a giant natural game reserve. Before man arrived the territory belonged to Africa's wild beasts and they roamed in huge numbers from the steaming heat of Tongaland to the cool Drakensberg. When the first Whites arrived in Natal, usually involuntary visitors dumped on the shores as shipwreck victims, they suffered at least as badly from attacks by animals as they did from attacks by hostile black tribes.

The first willing White settlers came to Natal largely because of the animals: there were so many elephants living in Natal that adventurers thought fortunes were to be made from the animals' ivory. It didn't work out like that, mostly because hunting elephants was not then an easy or safe proposition. Ivory, rather than being plentiful, was quite hard to come by and most of the early ivory traders went back home sadder and wiser men.

After Natal became a fully-fledged and well-settled colony under the British, weapons improved and the age of the hunter was born. It was considered absolutely *de rigueur* for an officer of the British army to blaze away at any animal unfortunate enough to wander anywhere within rifle range and the gallant officers competed furiously with one another to see who could bag the most animals.

Farmers were another trigger-happy lot. They hunted ferociously for the pot to eliminate predators which refused to distinguish between wild prey and domestic stock, and for fun. Thus the animals died in a blaze of rifle fire from Boer and Briton and today if you want to see wild animals in Natal it requires a journey to a nature reserve. Fortunately there are several good animal and bird reserves in the province.

Beginning in the north, there is the Ndumu Game Reserve in Tongaland, a 10 000 hectare reserve, one boundary of which actually borders Mozambique. Ndumu straddles the Usutu River and has a wealth of river life within its boundaries. It is estimated that at least 400 crocodiles live in the reserve and though that might seem a large number, in fact the authorities there are trying to breed more and have actually established a crocodile breeding station in the reserve. The baby crocodiles are protected for the first three years of their lives before being released into rivers.

Most people share the Zulu point of view which terms a crocodile *iNgwenya*, a 'lawless criminal,' but in fact they fulfil a very useful role in river ecology and are essential to African rivers. Poachers have wiped out an untold number of crocodiles as their skins are used for fashionable shoes and handbags, and fetch top prices on the open market.

Some 400 different species of birds have been spotted at Ndumu and the shallow river waters are particularly rich in aquatic bird life. The most notable feature of the reserve, though, is its trees, of which there are more than 200 different kinds set in a splendid natural forest. In the forest roam nyala, impala, duiker, bush pig, black and white rhinoceros, bushbuck and warthog but because the forest is dense it is not easy to see these animals. Hippopotami are also plentiful in the rivers of this reserve.

Further south in Tongaland is the Mkuzi Game Reserve, 25 091 hectares of natural parkland in which dwell impala, blue wildebeest, nyala, kudu, zebra, bushbuck, reedbuck, red and grey duiker, steenbok and black and white rhinos. It is also a haven for a rich variety of birdlife. Mkuzi was founded in 1912 but unfortunately periodic rumours surface that the area might be turned over to agriculture.

Almost due east of Mkuzi on the Tongaland coast is the tiny Sordwana Bay National Park. There is some animal life in this area of forest-covered sand dunes but its principal attraction is as a camping ground for fishermen.

Further south, close to the Zululand border, is the St Lucia Game Reserve, a large complex system of river and sea-fed shallow lakes especially rich in bird and fish life. Water covers some 36 826 hectares and everywhere the water touches is a declared reserve plus all the land surrounding the water to a width of one kilometre. 400 hippos live in the reserve keeping company with an untold number of crocodiles and around 25 species of aquatic birds, including flamingoes, pelicans, herons, kingfishers and cormorants. Large shoals of fish live in the lakes and their presence attracts sharks and big game fish at the estuary. For this reason St Lucia is a very popular spot for fishermen.

Inland from St Lucia, within the borders of Zululand, lies the 23 067 hectare Hluhluwe Game Reserve. Hluhluwe remains today a paradise for animals. Here in densely forested valleys and thickly grassed hill slopes Africa's animals have always roamed safe from the guns of hunters. Before law proclaimed the area a game reserve, the hunters' guns were kept at bay by the presence of tsetse fly. These flys carry deadly diseases which they transmit through their bites. A man bitten by a tsetse fly can develop sleeping sickness and bitten domestic stock can contract *nagana*, a killing disease.

For many years all man's attempts to eradicate these flies failed, among them the vicious methods of exterminating all animals in game reserves in an effort to get rid of any creatures which could serve as a source of food for the tsetse. All this achieved was to make the tsetse flies move out of the reserves and start attacking domestic herds. In one year, between 1945 and 1946, more than 60 000 head of cattle died because of the tsetse fly in Zululand. Then experiments began in which areas affected by the flies were sprayed with DDT. This was so successful in eliminating the flies that by 1953 they were virtually wiped out in the entire Zululand area.

Fortunately for the animals in Hluhluwe, by the time the flies were exterminated their area had been declared as a reserve. Today black and white rhinos, buffalo, nyala, kudu, impala, waterbuck, giraffe, zebra, blue wildebeest, leopards, cheetahs and lions live in the area and can easily be seen throughout the year. In 1981 elephants were reintroduced into the reserve.

To the south of Hluhluwe is the Umfolozi Game Reserve. It is thanks to dedicated conservationists working in this 47 753 hectare wilderness that Africa still has white rhinos. Everywhere else in Africa this square-lipped rhino became rarer and rarer until it was on the point of extinction. At Umfolozi conservationists fought an almost unnoticed battle to preserve the species. They were so successful that they have now exported more than 500 of the creatures to other reserves to begin the monumental task of restocking Africa. Their own herd is maintained at around 750 animals.

White rhinos aren't really white, they are a dingy sort of grey; and what distinguishes them from black rhinos is their larger size and square-lipped appearance. Despite their five tons of weight and massive horns, white rhinos are not aggressive. When threatened they form a circle with the young in the centre and all their horns facing outwards. This passive protective measure only enables hunters to shoot them all the more easily and contributed to their rapid decline in numbers. Black rhinos are far more aggressive and are apt to charge suspected persecutors with terrifying suddenness and startling speed.

Rhinos, both black and white, are hunted for their horns which are believed by some people to have aphrodisiac properties. There is absolutely no truth in this story, which probably originated because of the phallic appearance of the horn, but so widespread has it become that rhino horns are now worth more than their weight in gold. It's a tribute to the power of public belief that buyers are prepared to lay out a small fortune for something which is nothing more than a mass of tightly packed fibres.

There seems to be some special animal magic working at Umfolozi because a seeming miracle restocked the area with lions after all Zululand's indigenous lions had been killed by hunters many, many years ago. In 1958 a male lion crossed into South Africa from Mozambique and started making his way south. Every step of his journey was haunted by trigger-happy hunters anxious to bag him as a trophy but somehow he eluded them and miraculously arrived at the Umfolozi Game Reserve where he settled. Even more wondrously a few years later he was joined by several lionesses who successfully made the same perilous journey. The reserve's present lion population descends directly from this strange arrival.

A feature of Natal is that little game and nature reserves are to be found dotted near many towns. At Eshowe, a part of the Dhlinza Forest within the precincts of the town has been made into a reserve and in it live duiker, bushbuck, wild pigs, monkeys and birds. No creatures dangerous to man live there so it is quite safe to stroll through the forest paths.

Another small reserve is the Enseleni Nature Reserve near Richards Bay. It is only 293 hectares but within its borders live a wide variety of antelopes, wildebeest and zebras and it is rich in plant and tree life.

The Umlalazi Nature Reserve near the tiny coastal hamlet of Umtunzini preserves a piece of the Zululand coast as it must have been before the White man settled and developed it. The land is mostly sand dunes thinly covered with grass, yet in this seemingly unpromising environment live a number of small buck and many birds. The river which gives the reserve its name is full of crocodiles.

In the south of Natal is the Oribi Gorge Nature Reserve, part of the spectacular gorge of the Umzimkulwana River. Tall sandstone cliffs tower over a dense forest where a surprising number of animals still dwell. Leopards live here preying off the baboons and small animals. The gorge itself is very beautiful and on the cliff tops there are a number of fine viewpoints of the river thousands of feet below.

In the Natal Midlands is the Kamberg Nature Reserve on the banks of the Mooi River, chiefly remarkable for being the home of the Royal Zulu

Port Natal, later called D'Urban, from the Berea, painted by George French Angas c. 1847. (Cape Archives)

cattle, a pure white herd which have been specially bred by successive Zulu kings. There is good trout fishing in this area.

Durban

Surfers band and sway on the warm, furling waves while on the shore brightly-garbed rickshaw pullers seemingly mimic the surfers, leaping and swaying to attract customers. On the beaches beautiful girls wearing the minimum the law allows soak up the sun while residents of the chic hotels which tower in a monumental row on the promenade stand on their balconies and look down to the girls, the surfers and the ships that queue in the deep sea beyond, waiting to enter the busy harbour. This is Durban, Natal's most populous city.

Historically Durban is a monument to man's determination to tame and develop the wilderness. Less than two hundred years ago, where Durban stands today was a lagoon surrounded by wild mangroves. Modern Durban is famed for two things: its fine port, the busiest in Southern Africa, and its unashamed attempts to provide every sort of diversion for holiday-makers. On the sea-front there are performing dolphins, a fun-fair, a snake-park, and an aquarium where sharks glare balefully through thick glass at the tasty human morsels they can't quite reach. There are coloured lights, fantasy creatures of painted concrete, instant hamburgers, neon signs, loud musical combos and candy floss.

In this same city there are also bowling greens adorned by elderly white-clad players with clipped British accents, and a Club so British that the Union Jack was reluctantly hauled down only a few years ago. There is the Edward Hotel where a liveried attendant swings open the doors of limousines with a slight, respectful bow to welcome South Africa's elite.

Then there is the yachting set. Durbanites have always been enthusiastic yachtsmen, and the marina is always crowded with expensive, beautiful craft. Every weekend regattas take place in the bay. Alongside the sleek Durban-based yachts there sometimes lie weather-beaten gypsy craft pausing in Durban to restock with essential items before moving on to the

West Street, Durban, decorated to celebrate the relief of Ladysmith. (Cape Archives)

next port on the round-the-world voyage.

Horse-racing is another Durban passion. South Africa's premier race, the Durban July, takes place in the city and attracts visitors from all over the country. It has by tradition become a social event as well as a horse race. The unspoken rule is that the ladies attempt to outdo each other in the daring or outlandishness of their attire. On every other day of the year horse-racing is considered more serious business by Durbanites. Local newspapers publish special daily turf guides and almost everyone indulges in a little flutter occasionally.

Durban is a relaxed city. It must be so, or else the holiday-makers wouldn't go there and that would be disastrous for the city finances. Elsewhere in South Africa a dour Calvinism decrees that weekends are solemn occasions, but it's impossible to be solemn in Durban where the sea waits so invitingly a few metres from your door and Durbanites have refused to go along with closed-down Sundays. In Durban, shops open on the Sabbath and the Sunday trip to the shopping mall has become an instant Durban tradition.

Durbanites like to get out and mingle. The city is full of places of entertainment featuring live musicians, English pub atmospheres and a non-stop flowing of beer and conviviality. It's holiday time 352 days a year in Durban and what was once no more than a sand-fronted lagoon on a desolate coast has been transformed into a gleaming white city where the sounds of revelry never stop.

The three best-known areas of Durban are the beachfront, where most of the tourist attractions are situated; the Berea, which is a long ridge of land overlooking the harbour; and the Bluff, another ridge which forms the southern arm of the harbour. Berea gained its name from a mission which was established there in 1835 when it was still a densely forested place where wild animals roamed. Today the Berea is completely tamed and even contains 20 hectares of carefully cultivated botanic gardens. The Bluff too has been tamed and built into a residential area with an imposing view of the city and harbour.

Durban's harbour was once a lagoon fronted by a sand bar and it took engineers years to work out how to deepen the entrance sufficiently to allow large ships to enter. When they finally did so by dredging, they found that they had solved one problem only to create another. The same process that deepened the harbour entrance robbed Durban's beaches of the fine golden sand which made them so attractive.

Recently an ambitious and costly venture has been decided upon to replace the lost sand by pumping new supplies from the sea bed. It is still untested but the citizens of Durban have announced that they are going to maintain their beaches no matter at what cost because of the danger of losing their tourist industry if they do not.

Durban is also home to a large percentage of Natal's Indian population. Indian people are now employed in almost every occupation in the city and there is an exclusively Indian campus at the University of Natal near by. Brightly decorated Hindu temples liven up the city's architecture, elegantly dressed Indian women waft along the streets in beautiful saris and the Indian trading tradition has ensured that a bustling bazaar operates, trading in everything from cloth to pungent spices for the curries that are to be found on every Durban menu.

South Coast

One of the first holiday-makers to discover the charms of Natal's South Coast was an eccentric Englishman called Charles Hamilton who vacationed there in 1864 as the guest of an African village.

"A comfortable hut was allotted to me. I wore skins of animals tied around my waist, in sufficient quantities for all the purposes of ordinary clothing; and large banana leaves were sewn together by the sympathising girls of the kraal to prevent the sun from scorching my back and shoulders."

For ten months Hamilton remained at the village on the banks of the Umzimkhulu river during which time he fished, feasted and lazed around. Then, no doubt singularly refreshed in mind and body, he returned to civilisation. Untold numbers of vacationers have followed in Hamilton's footsteps and if today the comfortable hut has been exchanged for an air-conditioned hotel, the animals skins for a bathing costume and the banana-leaf sun barrier for sun-tan lotion, not much else has changed. Fishing, feasting and lazing around are still the order of the day.

The South Coast's sub-tropical climate makes it ideal for such activities. In the words of a nineteenth century Natal geographer, Robert Mann, Natal "possesses the leading characteristics of a tropical climate in a subdued and pleasantly softened degree. This, combined with a beautiful coastline veined with rivers and streams, nearly all of them ending in sand-fringed lagoons, and a warm ocean in which to swim, sail or fish has made the South Coast South Africa's holiday playground."

The South Coast also boasts one of the most important dates in any angler's diary, the Sardine Run. Each year between the seventh and tenth of June, huge shoals of pilchards migrate northwards hugging the coast from Port St. Johns to Durban. These fish get so close to the shore in places that housewives often dash down to the beach with buckets to scoop out a supperful. In the wake of these shoals follow the game fish which are an angler's delight: barracuda, kingfish, salmon, mussel-crackers, skates, rays and sharks. The Sardine Run lasts for about a month and millions of the little fish are devoured by various predators but because each female lays about 100 000 eggs, fish numbers remain stable.

Settlements ranging in size from hamlets to thriving towns dot the entire length of the South

Coast and most of them have camping sites, caravan parks and hotels. Like everywhere else in Natal the English influence is very evident on the South Coast. There are even English sea-side towns commemorated here: the English towns of Margate, Ramsgate and Southport all have South Coast namesakes and the little Natal towns with their town halls, shop-lined streets, churches and neat suburban houses have a decidedly English flavour.

Sharks live in the Indian Ocean which is the front door to all these towns and it is good to know that nearly every settlement has a netted bathing area to keep the sharks out. However, bathing can be dangerous in unprotected areas; shark attacks do take place on the South Coast and sometimes even in shallow water.

Port Edward is Natal's southernmost town, just a short distance from the Transkei border. It's a pleasant spot, well off the beaten track, with a lovely beach. The strip of land from Port Edward to Port Shepstone is known as the lower South Coast and differs slightly from the rest of the coastal area. On the lower South Coast green, grassy plains predominate where elsewhere there is forest and the climate is more temperate with less humidity in summer.

Marina Beach, Southbroom and Ramsgate, all on the lower South Coast, are all little places with good beaches, safe bathing and small hotels. Margate is rather different. It is a very popular spot for young people, particularly from the Transvaal and Zimbabwe. It has seven good hotels, three caravan parks and a host of well-organised entertainments.

Port Shepstone, which marks the dividing line between the coast regions, is the main administrative centre on this portion of the Natal coast. It is also an important railway terminus and was at one time used as a harbour. Today a big lighthouse stands watch over the entrance flashing a beacon to the passing ships.

Each of the little communities from Port Shepstone to Durban has its own charms and curiosities while all offer the holiday-maker accommodation, bathing and fishing. Near Umzumber, for example, is a famous Zulu 'luck heap' where once the Zulu king Shaka and his warriors each placed a pebble to propitiate any spirits who might live in the area. The bark of the *mtwalume* trees which grow at Umtwalume is said to be a cure for dysentery. Pennington is the site of an official holiday residence for the Prime Ministers of South Africa. The holiday house, 'Botha Home', was specially built for General Louis Botha, the first Prime Minister of the Union of South Africa. Scottburgh, one of the more popular spots along the coast, has a miniature railway. Amanzimtoti is a fast-developing residential area partially owing to the fact that Durban is only 27 kilometres away. In addition to its sandy beaches it also has a nature reserve which offers good walking along nature trails.

Although the South Coast's tourist industry is a large one the area remains quite unspoilt and there are many attractive places where travellers still have

the delight of finding little-known spots seemingly tailored to their express design.

North Coast

Natal's North Coast is less developed than the coast below Durban. There are fewer settlements and the coastline is generally wilder. The North Coast stretches one hundred kilometres north from Durban to the Tugela River, its boundary with Zululand, and is roughly fifty kilometres wide along its entire length.

In the early days of White settlements in Natal the North Coast was too close to the Zulus for comfort and only the braver spirits ventured into the region. Ivory hunters and a few traders and adventurers were the first White inhabitants of the North Coast and it was only in the 1840s when a group of Mauritians settled there that the area was firmly placed on the map. The Mauritians noticed that the North Coast's hot and humid climate was similar to that of their own island and so they planted a few of their favourite Mauritian delights in their new home, including the lovely *casuarina, ponciana* and flame trees.

Trade with Mauritius was quite lively in those days and thanks to it the North Coast of Natal was introduced to a crop which was to have a profound impact on the entire province. In 1847 40 000 tons of low quality sugar-cane were auctioned off in Durban. Economic conditions in Natal at the time were depressed, and as many farmers were keen to experiment with the new crop, by the following year there were patches of it growing here and there all along the North Coast.

When a man called Ephraim Rathbone arrived in Natal in 1848 from Mauritius to become overseer at an experimental cotton farm on the North Coast he noticed on his journey from Durban that the low-quality sugar-cane imported from Mauritius seemed to be growing well. He persuaded the manager of the cotton farm, Edmund Morewood, to plant an experimental patch of the cane on the cotton estate. Morewood became convinced that sugar-cane was the crop for the North Coast and in the following year he quit the foundering cotton venture to begin sugar-cane farming on his own at a place called Compensation.

In 1851 Morewood crushed a small crop of sugar in a mill he had built himself. His sugar was an immediate success and people flocked to him from all over Natal to learn the techniques of sugar production. Sugar can become a crop of vital importance for Natal as a whole and for the North Coast in particular. Today the sugar-cane industry produces more than two million tons of sugar every year and the first thing any visitor to the North Coast notices are the green cane fields marching away from the coast over the low hills.

Sugar is such an important crop to Natal that the sugar-cane estate owners are men of great influence. In 1860 a farmer called Liege Hulett began to grow sugar on the North Coast in a place called Mount Moreland. Today the Hulett family name is virtually a synonym for sugar in South Africa. In their hands and the hands of others like them rests an industry which generates employment for tens of thousands of people and earns millions of rands each year for the Republic of South Africa.

Other crops which have become economically important to the area are litchis, paw-paws and bananas. The exotic fruits grow so well on the North Coast that they compete favourably with fruit grown anywhere in the world and South Africans enjoy these splendid delicacies at low prices which would astound an overseas buyer.

Tourism is not such a major factor along the North Coast as it is to the south of Durban but Umhlanga Rocks, a town so close to the city as to be in danger of being swallowed by it, has a very sophisticated holiday centre. There are several luxury high-rise hotels, some first-rate restaurants and a beach made safe for swimming by shark nets and vigilant life guards.

Once past Umhlanga Rocks the atmosphere changes quickly. A modern highway runs north slightly inland from the coast. All along it signposts point seaward to places with names such as Compensation, Thompson's Beach, Sinkwazi Beach and Blythedale. Often the places indicated by the signposts are nothing more than wild sandy beaches fronted by rolling breakers and a few holiday houses. Along great stretches of coast no settlements exist at all, though here and there holiday spots do exist. Shaka's Rock (so called because it is believed that the Zulu King used it as a look-out point) has a small hotel, as do Salt Rock, Tongaat Beach and Mdloti.

The North Coast's principal towns are stretched out along the old main road which runs inland of the highway and here as everywhere else in the Garden Province, the English influence is felt. Mount Edgecombe was named after Mount Edgecumbe in Cornwall; Verulam further north was named after an English earl and Tongaat, a town which exists to process sugar-cane, has a village green complete with a cricket pitch which would not be out of place in any English village.

Stanger, the North Coast's busiest town, was named after William Stanger, the Surveyor-General of Natal, but it also has strong links with Shaka, the greatest Zulu King. It was here that Shaka built his last great capital, kwaDukuza, 'the place of he who was lost' so called because of the maze of passages between the huts, and it was here in 1828 that Shaka was assassinated by two of his half-brothers. Dingane, one of the assassins, went on to take the throne and to lead the Zulu people into disastrous conflict with the White Natal settlers.

The inland hills of the North Coast still have the timeless quality of unspoilt Africa. Few names appear on the maps but every one of the dirt roads winds past kraal after kraal, occasionally bisecting a little town with a few dusty stores and a petrol pump.

The North Coast's boundary is Natal's major river, the Tugela. The river rises in the far-off Drakensberg and by the time it reaches the sea it truly warrants its Zulu name, *Thukela*, 'something that startles'. In early days the Tugela was a serious obstacle to travellers and when it was flooded they were often prevented from crossing it for days at a time. Today the river is spanned by the 450-metre John Ross Bridge.

John Ross was a 15-year-old boy who in 1827 walked 900 kilometres from Durban to Mozambique and back in six weeks to obtain much-needed medicines. In those days there wasn't even a footpath along the coast and the route teemed with dangerous animals, snakes and crocodiles and with even more dangerous Zulu warriors. His safe return amazed even the adults who had despatched him on his mission.

Five kilometres before the John Ross Bridge is a turn-off which leads to the mouth of the Tugela where it finally meets the sea. This road passes the earliest river crossing point, Lower Tugela Drift, and the famous wild fig tree known as Ultimatum Tree.

Under this tree on 11th December, 1878, the British and the Zulus sat down together to discuss the future of Zululand and it was here that Cetshwayo's advisers heard the British demand concessions which they knew their king could never make. The discussions held under the shade granted by Ultimatum Tree led directly to the Zulu war and to the deaths of tens of thousands of people.

Drakensberg

Hundreds of millions of years ago a huge convulsion of the earth precipitated a great outpouring of lava from the point where Lesotho lies today. So much lava oozed from the earth's interior that it formed a layer 1 370 metres thick in places, which stretched more than 200 kilometres eastward to the sea. Erosion ate away at the soft basalt rock formed from the hardened lava and, moving at an average speed of one centimetre every six-and-a-half years, in only 140 million years cleared the broad strip of land which is present-day coastal Natal. To the west of this strip, however, the erosion process worked much more slowly and the result is that the remnants of that great lava flow can still be seen today in the shape of the Drakensberg mountains.

They run in a strip shaped like a crescent bulged eastwards for more than 200 kilometres, forming an almost unbroken barrier wall on Natal's western boundary with Lesotho. The mountains are justly famous for their beauty. Climbers make pilgrimages to test themselves on their peaks, ramblers find peace and solitude on their foothills and families visit them in winter to show children one of the few places in

South Africa where snow lies deep on the ground. The Drakensberg are romantic places. In a mapped world they are still partially unknown, where even the latest information says only that some peaks are unnamed and areas exist where dragons were once believed to live.

The Drakensberg mountains occupy a strip of land ranging from ten to sixteen kilometres in width and maintain an average altitude of 2 900 metres. They are undeniably impressive. Viewed from below they resemble a huge wall hundreds of metres high, topped here and there by jagged peaks. Natal's African inhabitants call the Drakensberg a 'wall of spears'.

The mountains are important as a rainfall catchment area and their ecological fragility is such that no agriculture or other activity which might upset the natural balance is permitted. Thus most of the Drakensberg has been proclaimed a wilderness and recreational area. Even recreational use is limited and a person who enters the wilderness area "must depend for survival upon his own resources and on what food and shelter he can carry on his back," as the Natal Regional Planning Commission put it in a report made about the mountains.

The Drakensberg is divided into two distinct areas. The tops of the mountains are called the High Berg while grass-covered finger-like spurs which project into Natal are called the Little Berg. At the summit of the mountains runs a high plateau which is often called the 'Roof of Africa'. The edge of the plateau is riven with rocky passes and steep grass slopes. This terrain gives way to the Little Berg which terminate in a line of conspicuous yellow sandstone cliffs running the entire length of the mountain range.

The first human inhabitants of the Drakensberg were Bushmen who took up residency some 8 000 years ago. The Bushmen were simple people who sheltered in caves and lived on what prey they could kill with their light bows and arrows. When the Bantu people arrived in Natal in the seventeenth century they quickly forced the Bushmen to retreat to the higher, more inaccessible regions of the mountains. The rise of Shaka's Zulu empire sent so many refugees scurrying through the Drakensberg's mountain passes that the area became depopulated again and for a brief period the Bushmen lived unmolested. Then the Voortrekkers arrived and the days of the Bushmen were numbered.

The trekkers created farms on the foothills and the hunters moved into the higher regions and started shooting out the game. The Bushmen who depended on the animals for their very existence retaliated by descending on the farms below and hunting any animal they could find, making no distinction between wild and domestic creatures. The farmers responded by declaring the Bushmen to be 'vermin' and organising hunting parties to exterminate them.

By 1890 the last of the Bushmen were dead, leaving behind them a wonderful legacy in the rock paintings they made. More than 19 000 of these paintings have been discovered and they include some of the finest examples of the art existing in the world. The Bushmen took their subject matter from the things they saw around them; most of the pictures depict animals, particularly eland and grey rhebuck. Where humans are portrayed they are invariably in motion— hunting, running or, in later periods, fighting with men, both black and white. There are even scenes of red-coated soldiers on horseback dating from the time of the British occupation of Natal.

Nothing is known of the individuals who made the paintings although experts claim to be able to follow the work of individual artists from site to site. It is recorded that the last great Bushmen artist was shot dead in 1866. On his body was found a belt to which were attached ten antelope horns, each filled with a different pigment, his equivalent of an artist's palette.

The animals which the Bushmen painted survived their recorders: eland and grey rhebuck still roam the Drakensberg although mainly in designated game reserves. Generally there is an abundance of bird, reptile and animal life in the mountains. Leopards live in the high, remote areas preying on the smaller animals which still exist there. There are numerous varieties of birds and snakes. Some of the snakes are deadly poisonous and visitors are advised always to be on the look-out for them.

The greatest dangers in the Drakensberg, though, are the mountains themselves. The basalt which forms them is soft and crumbly, as many a climber has found to his cost. The peaks have to be treated with great respect, a factor which only serves to enhance their attraction in the eyes of the dedicated.

For management purposes the Natal Drakensberg has been divided into seven different regions. In the far north is the Royal Natal National Park where a hill called Mount-aux-Sources is the source of five rivers: the Eastern and Western Khubedu, both tributaries of the Orange River; the Elands, which flows into the Orange Free State; the Bilanjil and the Tugela. These last two rivers flow into Natal, plunging over the edge of another famous landmark, a crescent-shaped rock wall called the Amphitheatre which rises 500 metres above the Little Berg. This waterfall, called the Tugela Falls, plunges 850 metres in five clear leaps and is one of the highest in the world.

The Royal Natal National Park also contains some magnificent free-standing peaks, including the Sentinel (3 166 metres) which in 1910 was one of the first peaks in the Drakensberg to be climbed; and Devil's Tooth (2 941 metres) which in 1950 was one of the last to be conquered. For those who find their pleasure in rambling, the park contains about 130 kilometres of good paths and walkers can visit Bushman paintings, fish for trout or watch for game which is abundant in the area.

Next to the Royal Natal National Park is the Singati, Mnweni area. This is one of the least well-known areas of the mountains largely because of its inaccessibility. Dogged spirits who don't mind awful roads and the prospect of progress being barred in summer months by swollen streams, are rewarded on reaching the High Berg by some of the finest scenery anywhere along the mountain range.

African people named this area *Mnweni*, 'the place

of the fingers', because of spires of rock which stand up like the fingers of a hand. Mnweni Castle (3 117 metres) has been called the loveliest of all the Drakensberg peaks and on its western slopes can be found the true source of the Orange River. Immediately south of Mnweni Castle is the single largest rock mass in the whole of the Drakensberg, the 3 145 metre Saddle, so called because it is shaped like the saddle of a horse.

Moving south one comes to an area known by one of its most famous mountains, Cathedral Peak. This 3 004 metre mountain is one of the favourite climbs in the Drakensberg because it is accessible to anyone with the stamina for a stenuous walk. The final ascent to the summit is made easier by the provision of a short chain ladder. The view from the top is splendid in every direction. There are other fine peaks in the area but they all require varying degrees of climbing skill. The Cathedral Peak area is great walking country and a network of paths criss-crosses the lower slopes of the mountains leading to forests and swimming holes, waterfalls and Bushman paintings. There is even a hotel close enough to make the possibility of a hot bath a reality at day's end.

Further south still lies the Mdedelolo Wilderness Area, a vast and rugged area that takes its name from a huge, brooding mountain the African people call *Mdedelolo*. Mdedelolo means 'make way for him' and is the Zulu name for a bully. Less picturesquely the mountain's English name is Cathkin Peak, named after a mountain near the Scottish home of a pioneer farmer. The Mdedelolo area is full of good climbs, such as Monk's Cowl (3 234 metres), one of the most difficult Drakensberg peaks; Sterkhorn (2 973 metres) which has a memorial to the dead of World War II on the summit; Intunja (2 408 metres) and Champagne Castle (3 377 metres), so called because the British climbers who first set out to conquer it took with them a bottle of champagne to drink when they reached the summit. They gave up before they reached the top so decided to open the bottle anyway. When they unpacked it they found it was half empty. Both climbers swore they hadn't touched a drop so they decided the mountain had taken it – hence 'Champagne Castle'. There is good walking in this district too but for the enthusiast with a few days to spare, the trails are long and very wild.

A few kilometres south of Champagne Castle, jutting out some three kilometres from the main escarpment, lies the most obvious prominence in the entire Natal Drakensberg. The English name of this 3 314 metre mountain is Giant's Castle but the Zulus call it *Ntabayikonwa*, 'the mountain at which one must not point', because they believe that to do so brings bad weather. The mountain lends its name to the entire area surrounding it, The Giant's Castle Game Reserve, and it is one of the most popular areas of the entire range. The High Berg forms three, long unbroken stretches of rock wall at this point: the Red Wall, the Trojan Wall and the Long Wall.

The area boasts the highest point in South Africa, the Injasuti Dome (3 379 metres) and ten kilometres to the west, in Lesotho territory, the second highest

point in Southern Africa, Makheke (3 461 metres). The area also holds a memorable place in Natal's history. In 1873 the British were very concerned about the fact that Natal tribesmen were acquiring firearms. They demanded that these be surrendered and when a chieftan called Langilabalele refused to hand his over, an order was issued that he be arrested. Langilabalele and his people promptly fled up the mountain, making their escape via a pass then known as Bushman's River Pass.

Major Anthony Durnford was placed in command of a British force and charged with driving Langilabalele's people back to Natal. The British plan called for Durnford and his men to climb two passes adjacent to Bushman's River Pass and to block off Langilabalele's escape route. One pass proved non-existent and the other, Giant's Castle Pass, required mountaineering skills to pass through it. The climb was a nightmare for Durnford's party. It took them a whole night to reach the top. They were exhausted when they finally did so and Durnford had injured an arm so severely that he never recovered its use. To make matters worse, when Langilabalele's people began to emerge from their pass, they first made it clear they were not prepared to return to Natal and then attacked Durnford's party, killing several men.

Durnford was forced to make a hasty retreat back down the pass he had laboured so hard to climb. Langilabalele got clean away. After that eventful night Bushman's River Pass was renamed Langilabalele's Pass and the bloody little skirmish is further commemorated by a memorial cross on the summit.

More peaceful times reign now and the area is one of the best along the entire range for bird and game viewing. It also has an abundance of Bushman art including some of the finest specimens in all Africa.

Adjoining the Giant's Castle Game Reserve is the Umkhomazi Wilderness Area. This area, which is less well-known than some of the northern parts of the range, offers spectacular scenery and a spectacularly bad road which crosses into Lesotho. The drive through Sani Pass offers unrivalled views but road conditions are so bad that it is restricted to four-wheel-drive vehicles. Five kilometres from the escarpment edge, in Lesotho territory, lies the highest point in Southern Africa, Thaba Ntlenyana (3 482 metres) - 'The Beautiful Little Mountain'. It is a measure of the wildness of this area that several peaks of over 3 000 metres are still nameless and virtually unknown.

South of Sani Pass the escarpment swings sharply southwest to the Umzimkulu Wilderness Area. The mountains in this area are as little known as those in Umkhomazi and are often nameless. One that is named, Hodgson's Peak, is the subject of a macabre little incident. It is named for a certain Thomas Hodgson who was accidentally shot by one of his companions during a raid against the Bushmen. The incident took place in thick mist and the party, fearful of a Bushman attack, buried Hodgson with great haste. Only when they had safely returned to Natal did members of the party voice their suspicions that Hodgson had not been dead when they buried him.

There is good walking in this area and the Little Berg has some unusually beautiful buttresses and rock formations.

The Drakensberg can be visited all the year round but visibility is often better in the winter. The winter climate is typefied by warm to cool sunny days and very cold nights. Snow falls six to twelve times a year. In summer the days are hot and nights warm or coolish, and rainfall is frequent and heavy.

Midlands

The interior of Natal is a very different world from the coastal regions. There the sea dominates and the towns stretch alongside it in a narrow, busy strip. To the inhabitants of the 200 kilometre-broad Natal Midlands, Natal's coastal inhabitants are people who are always in a hurry, preoccupied with the brief visits of ships and 'planes and the needs of tourists. The folk of the Midlands, citizens of such towns as Colenso or Vryheid or even of Pietermaritzburg itself, shake their heads in wonderment at the pace of life at the coast. In the Midlands life is slower, naturally so because much of it is centered around crops and cattle and the steady changing of the seasons.

Many South Africans known little of the Midlands of Natal except the towns which line the route from Johannesburg to the sea: Estcourt, Colenso, Ladysmith and the famous Van Reenen's Pass, a road through the Drakensberg so steep and baffling to the engineers that they never seem satisfied with their latest attempt to tame it. The roadside always seems marked with the beginnings of ambitious new ventures to make the passage through the mountains ever safer and speedier.

If one pauses at the top of Van Reenen's Pass and looks down into the depths where the road plunges, it seems amazing that a road should exist there at all, so awesomely and suddenly does the land fall away. Another route through the Midlands to the coast does exist via Newcastle and Ladysmith but it is longer and narrower and therefore less popular with the majority of travellers who wish only to get to the sea as fast as possible.

Those that hurry through the Natal Midlands miss a great deal; the broad band of land contains a world of charm and beauty. The soil of the Midlands is fertile and the towns which grew up here did so mostly to serve the needs of farming communities. Pietermaritzburg, the central city of the Midlands, was itself founded by Boer farmers in the days when they challenged the British for the right to rule Natal and they chose the site of their capital city with farming in mind: the soil is good, water is plentiful and the climate is mild. The Boers named their city after two of their leaders, Piet Retief and Gert

Maritz, and settled down to create their dream of a Boer Republic.

Only for a few years did that dream endure and then in 1843 the British took possession of Pietermaritzburg and turned it into a garrison town and the seat of their administration in Natal. The new arrivals imported to the city an English flavour which lingers still. Natal's first newspaper, the *Natal Witness,* was published in Pietermaritzburg. It still rolls off the presses every morning with news of the bowling competitions and cattle shows. In 1893 the British built a massive Victorian city hall and although it was burned down in 1895 it has been rebuilt and dominates the city's main street.

The early citizens of Pietermaritzburg were far-sighted enough to lay out parks and gardens in their city. Some of the more impressive are the Mayor's Garden, a five-hectare rock garden; Wylie Park, eight hectares devoted to a collection of trees from all over the world, and Alexandra Park, which covers 44,5 hectares and has sports fields as well as gardens. The University of Natal has a campus in Pietermaritzburg which is well-known for the high standard of its agricultural degrees.

The term Natal Midlands is applied to a long stretch of land from Kokstad on the border with Transkei in the south to Volksrust near the Swazi border in the north. Agriculture is the principal occupation of many of the people who live between these two points but it is by no means the area's only industry. Coal is mined in the Dundee/Newcastle areas and there is a steel works at Newcastle. A timber and wattle bark industry has been established around Greytown. Paper is made from the trees and tannic acid found in the bark is used in the leather-tanning industry. Estcourt has become a centre for the processing of farm products, particularly meat and milk.

The Midlands also possesses some of the finest private schools in South Africa. Michaelhouse at Balgowan and Hilton College at Hilton are both exclusive schools with world-wide reputations. St. Anne's at Hilton and Epworth in Pietermaritzburg are girls' schools with equally high reputations. Teverton School outside Mooi River has built up an outstanding reputation as a school which develops musical ability.

Many of the towns and landmarks of the Midlands have fascinating histories. Kokstad, for example, was founded by a Griqua chief called Adam Kok who led his people there in the early 1860s from the Orange Free State because he had heard it was a promised land. In a way it was, because the land proved ideal for agriculture, but sadly most of the Griquas sold the land they were allocated and squandered the money they were paid. An oddity of this area is that shortly after it leaves Kokstad the main road leading to Pietermaritzburg passes through a segment of the independent country of Transkei which is entirely cut off from the rest of Transkei territory and exists as an island of foreign soil completely surrounded by Natal.

Richmond is the home of the Bhaca people whose

intricately beaded costumes are amongst the most colourful in Africa. The existence of the Bhaca people is a result of the days when the Zulus ruled Natal. Their names mean 'the people who hide' and they were formed from the remnants of tribes who fled from the Zulu tyranny.

Ladysmith was the scene of a famous military seige during the Boer war when a small British garrison held out against superior Boer forces.

Utrecht was once the capital of one of the world's smallest republics when in 1854 a group of cattle-ranchers declared themselves independent and ruled an area 32 kilometres by 64 kilometres as a sovereign state. Law and order was enforced by the leader's wife, a woman famed for her strength and wrestling abilities.

Vryheid also briefly was the capital of a country, one formed by mercenary soldiers who had helped to put Dinuzulu on the Zulu throne in 1884. The mercenaries' republic might have had some chance of

survival because it seemed that the German government was interested in helping them – to their own ends of course – but the British quickly intervened to protect their national interest and the Republic died.

Spioenkop is a Midlands mountain notable for two reasons. It was the scene of a famous Boer victory during the Anglo-Boer war and on its slopes rises the Umgeni River, one of the most important Natal rivers. On its way eastward to the sea the Umgeni feeds the Midmar Dam, drives a hydro-electric plant at Howick, tumbles attractively over the Howick and the Albert Falls and then flows for 64 kilometres between Pietermaritzburg and Durban through the Valley of a Thousand Hills. This imposing, deeply-eroded valley is a well-known beauty spot for Midlands visitors. Its lovely surroundings give the visitor no hint of evil but the area was once the haunt of cannibal tribes and for many years strangers in the area went in mortal fear of being eaten.

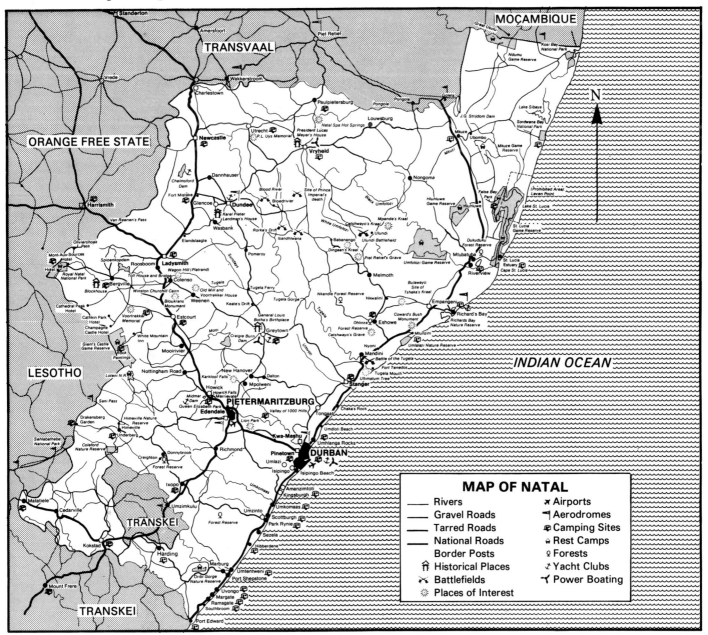

MAP OF NATAL

—— Rivers	✈ Airports
—— Gravel Roads	⊣ Aerodromes
—— Tarred Roads	🏕 Camping Sites
—— National Roads	⛺ Rest Camps
Border Posts	♀ Forests
⛪ Historical Places	⚓ Yacht Clubs
Battlefields	⌃ Power Boating
Places of Interest	

2 The Tugela River, near its source in the Royal Natal National Park.

3 Looking toward the Amphitheatre in the Royal Natal National Park. Although small, this park is probably the best known part of the Natal Drakensberg.

Two further scenes of the Royal Natal National Park:

4 High up the Tugela River, below Mont-aux-Sources.

5 A natural swimming pool near the camp site in the park.

6

7

6 Farming landscape near the Royal
Natal National Park.

7 The sheer walls of the Amphitheatre.

8

9

8 A summer landscape within the park itself.

9 View towards the Eastern Buttress and Devil's Tooth of the Amphitheatre.

10

12

10 Mountain forest growing in the Royal Natal National Park.

11 Attractively situated, the park's Tendele hutted camp is extremely popular with holiday-makers and climbers.

12 The crescent-shaped Amphitheatre is the central feature of the park. From left to right: Eastern Buttress, Amphitheatre Wall, Beacon Buttress and Sentinel – with the Tugela River in the foreground.

11

14

13 The eastern side of the Amphitheatre, showing from left to right: Eastern Buttress, Devil's Tooth, Inner Tower, Mt. Amery and the Amphitheatre Wall.

14 Hikers gathering outside the Mont-aux-Sources Hotel. Walks are organised into the Drakensberg by the Natal Parks Board and the local hotels.

15 The western peak of the Amphitheatre, the Sentinel.

16 Overleaf: Cathedral Peak.

15

17

18

19

17 Champagne Castle, seen from the hotel grounds.

18 Basket weaving in the Champagne Castle area.

19 Horses at Champagne Castle.

Some flowers of the Natal Drakensberg:

20 *Apodolirion*, flowering in October.

21 *Hesperantha schelpiana*.

20

21

22

23

24

22 *Helichrysum adenocarpum*, an everlasting species.

23 *Helichrysum squarrosum*.

24 *Greyia sutherlandii*, the Natal bottlebrush.

25

25 Drakensberg landscape in the Giant's Castle Game Reserve.

26 Zulu huts near Cathedral Peak.

27 An eland bull in the Giant's Castle Game Reserve. This reserve is the best area in the Drakensberg for game and bird watching.

28 Overleaf: Giant's Castle, covered in snow.

26

29

30

31

29-30 Giant's Castle is unsurpassed as an area for Bushman rock art. These examples were photographed in the Main Caves.

31 The Bushman Cave Museum at Main Caves.

32 Another majestic Drakensberg landscape in the Giant's Castle area.

32

33 In summer the Drakensberg foothills change to a beautiful shade of green.

34

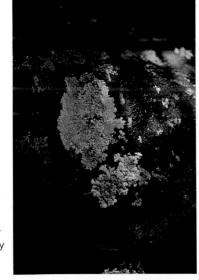

35

34 The spectacular Sani Pass, the only road access to Lesotho from the east.

35 Tree lichen in a Drakensberg forest.

36 A farm near Underberg, the gateway to the southern regions of the Natal Drakensberg.

36

Leaving the Drakensberg we now enter the Midlands which lie between the Drakensberg and the coast:

37 Sugar cane plantations and Zulu huts near Greytown.

38 *Aloe saponaria* blooms in August in the Natal Midlands.

38

39

39 The Soofie Mosque and Madressa – a beautiful example of Muslim architecture found at Ladysmith.

40 A view of Ladysmith from Wagon Hill.

41 Sugar cane plantations near Greytown.

42 An evening scene near Newcastle.

43 Overleaf: Bales of wheat harvested near Van Reenen's Pass.

40

41

42

44

45

46

44 Farm landscape near Greytown.

45 The countryside near Nottingham Road.

46 The Umgeni Valley near Howick.

47 The Howick Falls, over which the water of the Umgeni flows.

47

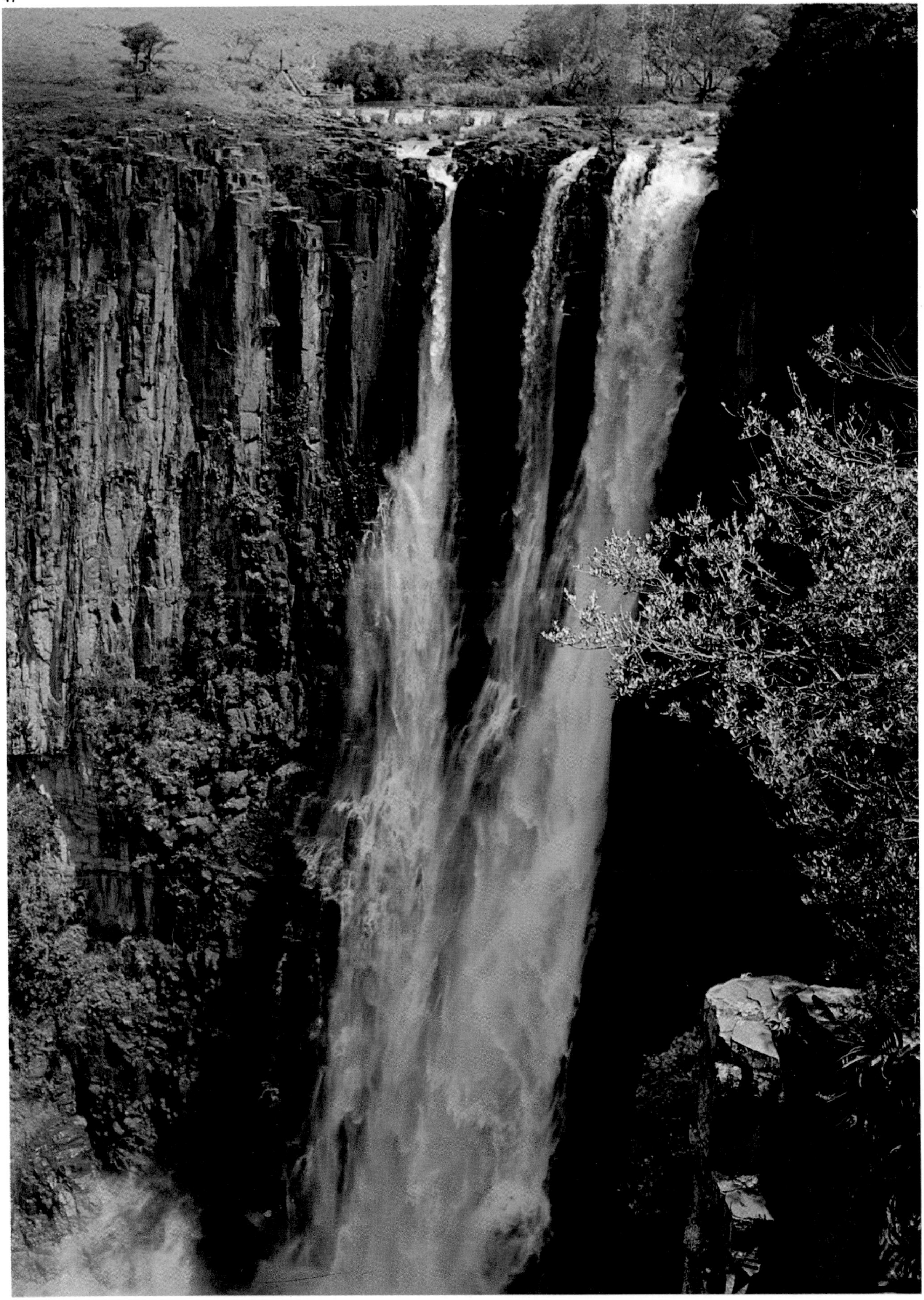

48 Zulu dwellings in the Valley of a Thousand Hills.

49 The Karkloof Falls, near Howick.

52

Historical landmarks in Pietermaritzburg:

53 Zulu War Memorial.

54 The oldest surviving house in Pietermaritzburg.

55-56 The Church of the Vow and the Vow made by the Voortrekkers before the Battle of Blood River.

54

55

56

Some facets of Pietermaritzburg:

57 Shoppers.

58 The City Hall.

59 The Old Pavilion and Bandstand.

60 The head office of the Natal Parks Board at the Queen Elizabeth Park.

61 Midmar Dam, a favourite weekend haunt.

59

60

61

62

63

The Natal South Coast stretches along the Indian Ocean coastline from Durban to the Transkei. It is one of South Africa's prime recreational areas:

62 Margate, one of the most popular resorts on the lower South Coast.

63 The narrow-guage railway which runs inland from Umzinto to Ixopo.

64 The Zulu Market, near Durban, on the South Coast road.

65 One of the colourful stalls at the Zulu Market.

66 Lagoon and sea divided by a narrow stretch of beach at Southbroom.

67 Overleaf: Ramsgate Lagoon, late afternoon.

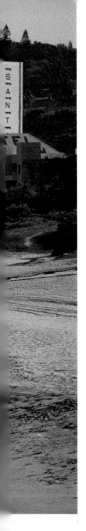

64

65

66

68 Bathers at Amanzimtoti.

69 Scottburgh.

70 Oribi Gorge, one of the great scenic attractions of the south.

71 A flower of the kaffirboom or coral tree, *Erythrina caffra*.

72 The Umzimkulwana River, flowing through Oribi Gorge.

73 Scene near Ixopo.

70

71

72

73

74 Durban harbour, as seen from the Bluff, at night.

74

75 The Elangeni and Maharani, two of Durban's most prestigious hotels.

75

76

Some of Durban's colourful people:

76 A Zulu Rickshaw Boy, with the Malibu Hotel in the background.

77 A Moslem prayer leader at the Grey Street Mosque.

78 The flower market.

79 A Hindu wedding ceremony.

80 Overleaf: A yacht sailing off Durban, one of the two main yachting centres of South Africa.

77

81

82

Further scenes of Durban:

81 Walking tall in Minitown, on the beachfront. The replicas are in 1-in-24 scale.

82 The Grey Street Mosque.

83 A curry stall in the Indian Market.

84 Staff members of the Maharani, one of Durban's two five-star hotels.

83

84

85 Warm waters, protected from sharks – one of Durban's chief attractions.

86 Durban beachfront, with its amusement parks and high-rise holiday flats and hotels.

87 Natal is the hub of South African horse-racing and the Rothmans July Handicap is the country's premier race.

86

87

88
89

88 The Orchid House in the Durban Botanical Gardens houses over 3 000 plants.

89 The lighthouse at Umhlanga Rocks.

90 The beach at Umhlanga Rocks, with the Cabanas nearest the camera.

91

92

Scenes from Southern Zululand, north of Durban:

91 Mangroves growing in the Umlalazi Nature Reserve near Mtunzini.

92 A corner of the Dhlinza Forest Reserve, Eshowe.

93 Sugar cane in the foreground with Empangeni in the background.

94 Harvesting sugar cane near Hluhluwe.

93

94

95 The Enseleni River and Nature Reserve near Empangeni.

96 Fort Nongquai, Eshowe.

97 Cape honeysuckle, *Tecomaria capensis*, in bloom in Zululand in August.

97

95

96

98 A bush-baby in the Nyala Game Ranch, near Empangeni.

99 A cheetah in a private Zululand game reserve.

100 Richards Bay at sunset.

101 Natal wild plum, *Carissa macrocarpa*.

101

102 This portrait of a Zulu headman introduces the Zulu section of the book.

103 A Zulu witchdoctor consulting the bones outside his traditional hut.

104 A Zulu woman washing clothes in the Tugela River.

105 The Mooi River, a tributary of the Tugela, at Keate's Drift.

108

106 Proud but not arrogant, this beautiful woman and her baby were photographed near Tugela Ferry.

107 Like most African people, the Zulus love music and dancing.

108 An elderly induna smoking his pipe outside the cattle kraal.

109 A young girl minding a stall at Keate's Drift.

110 Overleaf: Oxen pulling a sledge along a dusty Zululand road.

109

107

111 A Zulu kraal situated between Tugela Ferry and Keate's Drift.

112 Another kraal, near Vryheid.

113 A Zulu couple outside a trading post near Tugela Ferry.

114 Zulu girls.

115

116

115 A sledge laden with mielie meal, fording a stream near Hlabisa, south of Nongoma.

116 This study of a Zulu woman clearly illustrates the dress and jewellery of the Tugela Ferry area.

117

118

117 Zulu girls near Keate's Drift.
Compare their dress with that of the
married woman in the previous picture.

118 Young children outside their grass
hut.

119 Zulu huts near Pomeroy.

Several pictures in the Zulu section of
this book, including the two on this
page, were taken at an authentic Zulu
kraal near Nkwaleni. This kraal may be
visited by the public and courses in the
Zulu culture and language are also
offered:

120 The men display a traditional dance
at the kraal.

121 Relaxing in the shade of a thorn
tree.

122 Kwa-Zulu landscape near Draycott.

123 Zulu girls outside a trading store at Keate's Drift.

123

124 Scholars at a primary school in Kwa-Zulu.

125-127 A spearmaker hammers out the point of a spear, sharpens the blade and then inspects the finished product.

124

125

126

127

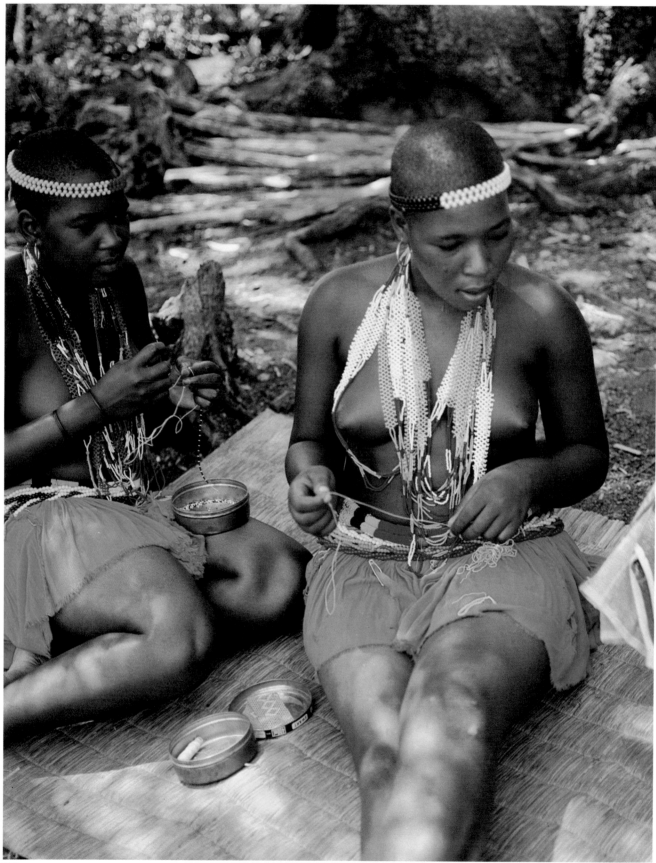

128 A young Zulu woman stringing beads.

129 Zulu women, in magnificent dress, with Isandhlwana in the background.

130

131

130 Zulu women selling fruit at Nongoma.

131 Kwa-Zulu landscape near Oliviershoek, with the Drakensberg in the background.

132

132 Cotton growing in Zululand.

133 A Zulu woman stitching a traditional goatskin skirt.

133

In Natal, where there was room for everybody, people paid for their land with blood. Boer against Zulu, Zulu against Briton, Briton against Boer – today monuments and graves remind us of these tragic confrontations:

134 The grave of Piet Retief and his followers near Dingane's Kraal.

135-136 Isandhlwana Battlefield. The white mounds of stones are graves – the ground was too hard to dig proper graves at the time.

137

138

137 The Burgher Monument at Wagon Hill, near Ladysmith.

138 The main plaque at the Burgher Monument.

139 A plaque at Rorke's Drift.

140 The graveyard at Rorke's Drift.

141 The site of the battle at Rorke's Drift.

139

140

141

142 A plaque at the memorial at Ulundi.

143 The memorial at Blood River.

144 British war graves at Wagon Hill, Ladysmith.

145 The war memorial at Ulundi.

143

IN MEMORY OF

THE BRAVE WARRIORS WHO FELL

HERE IN 1879 IN DEFENCE OF THE

OLD ZULU ORDER

146

147

Moving to a happier subject, we take a look at some of Zululand's famous game reserves:

146 The Black Umfolozi River – the northern boundary of the Umfolozi Game Reserve.

147 Lions in the reserve.

148 A white rhino against a magnificent backdrop of acacias.

149 Waterbuck cows in the riverine vegetation of the Umfolozi Game Reserve.

150 A warthog enjoys the mud at an Umfolozi waterhole.

151 Close-up of a white rhino in the reserve.

152 Zebra in the Umfolozi Game Reserve.

153 A kudu bull in the reserve.

154 Giraffe photographed from Umfolozi's Bekapanzi hide.

152

153

154

 155

156

155 This landscape shows the terrain so typical of the Hluhluwe Game Reserve.

156 Pied crow and white-backed vulture at a kill in Hluhluwe.

157 Nyala of both sexes at the reserve's Munywaneni waterhole.

157

Scenes in and around Hluhluwe Game Reserve:

158 A Zulu gatekeeper at the Zululand Safari Lodge on the Ubizane Game Ranch.

159 The Hluhluwe River.

160 Wild Iris, *Dietes iridioides*, in the reserve.

161 A Marico sunbird photographed in a weeping Boer-bean tree, *Schotia brachypetala*, in the reserve.

162 The swimming pool at the Hluhluwe Holiday Inn, presided over by a magnificent fever tree, *Acacia xanthophloea.*

163 A male lesser masked weaver starting to construct a nest in the Hluhluwe village.

164 Overleaf: Dawn, Hluhluwe Game Reserve.

161 160 162 163

165

166

167

165 Grey-headed gulls near the Lake St Lucia estuary.

166 Lesser flamingo on the lake.

167 The Natal Parks Board operates launch tours on the lake. Note the dense vegetation in the background.

169

170

171

Further aspects of Lake St Lucia:

168 The beach near the estuary.

169 Hippo in the lake.

170 Boating near the estuary.

171 Poacher's weapons on display.

172 The crocodile research station.

172

173 A Goliath heron at the lake's edge.

174 Tropical vegetation near the estuary.

175 Scene at Mkuzi Game Reserve.

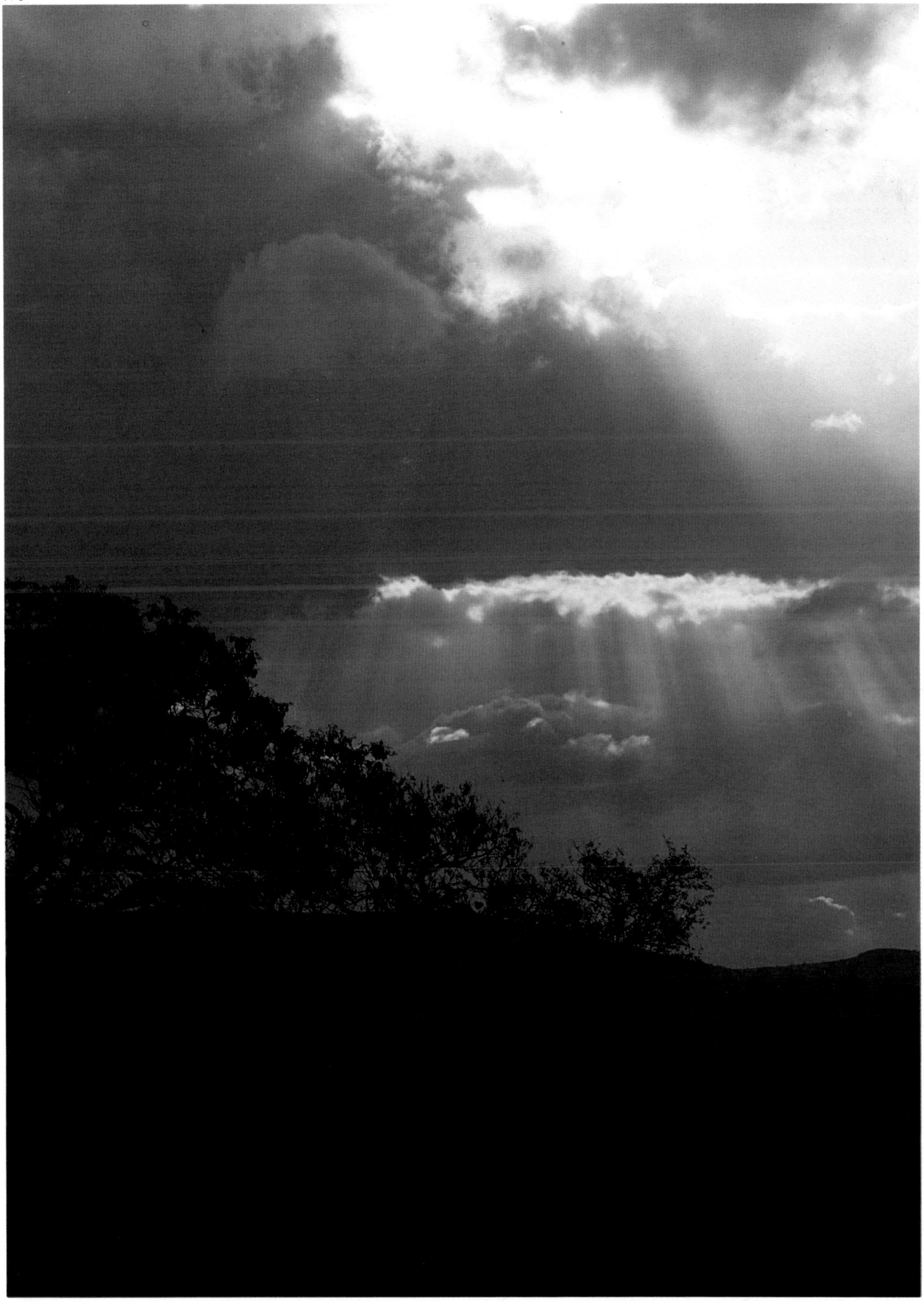

176 Ghost mountain, near Mkuzi village.

177 A wild fig, *Ficus sycamorus*, growing in the Mkuzi Game Reserve.

177

178 A white-backed vulture in the Mkuzi Game Reserve.

179 A baboon family drinking at Mkuzi.

180 Warthog drinking.

181 A nyala bull at the Msinga waterhole.

181

180

184

185

Some photographs taken at Mkuzi's two famous hides, Bube and Msinga:

182 A grey heron with a freshly-caught frog.

183 Blue wildebeest drinking while zebra await their turn.

184 Close-up of an impala ram drinking.

185 Close-up of a crocodile waiting . . .

186 White-faced whistling ducks on Ndumu's Nyamiti Pan.

187 Early morning at Ndumu.

186

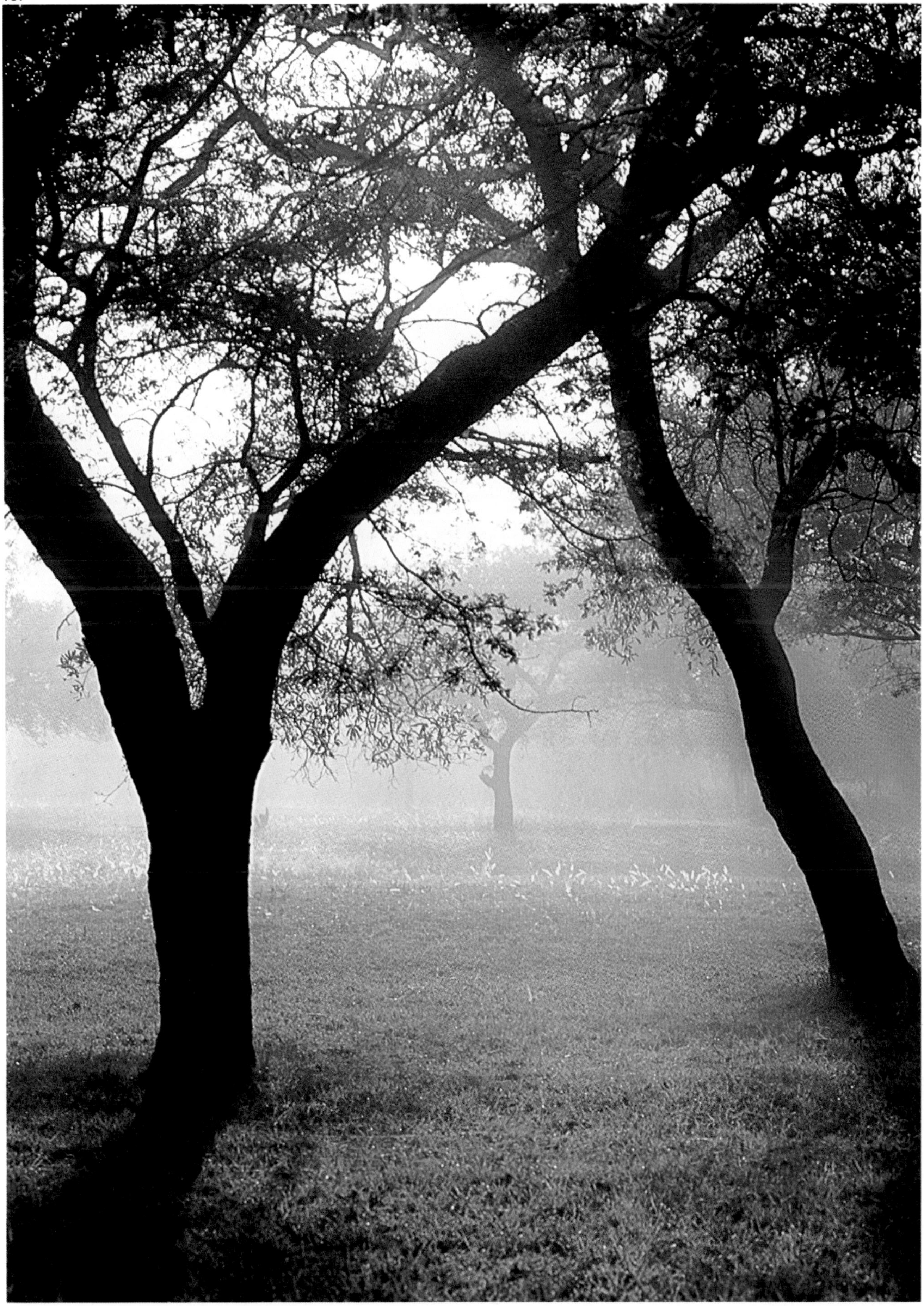

188 An orchid, *Ansilea gigantis*, growing in Ndumu.

189 The wild fig forest, *Ficus sycamorus*, alongside the Pongola River in Ndumu.

190 Nyamiti Pan.

191 Bird-watchers in the reserve.

192 A hippo in the Pongola River.

18

190

191

192

193 A road through the thick Ndumu bush, showing a nyala ewe in the distance.

194 Sordwana Bay National Park.

195 A Tonga girl and her sister.

195

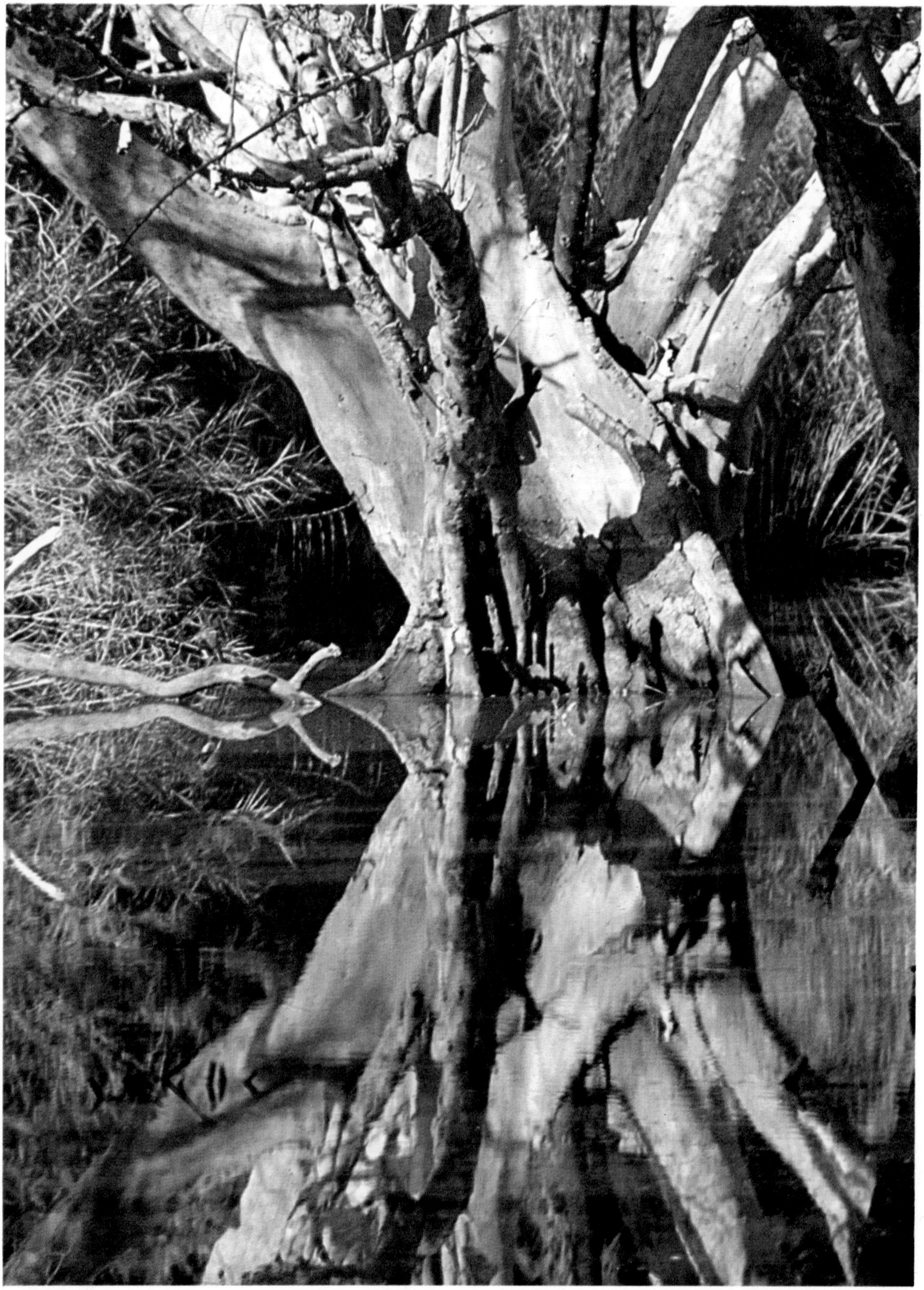

Tongaland kaleidoscope:

196 Reflections of a wild fig.

197 Tongaland landscape.

198 The road to Ndumu on market morning.

199 Overleaf: Natal sunset.

197

198